U.S. DEPARTMENT OF JUSTICE
OFFICE OF COMMUNITY ORIENTED POLICING SERVICES

METHAMPHETAMINE INITIATIVE

FINAL ENVIRONMENTAL ASSESSMENT

May 13, 2003

Table of Contents

1.0 Introduction

Clandestine drug laboratories are used in the illicit production of illegal drugs, most often methamphetamine, but also other types of illegal drugs. The Department of Justice (DOJ) Community Oriented Policing Services (COPS) Office Methamphetamine Initiative provides grant funding to state, local, Tribal, and other public (not Federal) law enforcement entities (referred to throughout this document as "state and local law enforcement agencies) for their methamphetamine initiatives. The state and local law enforcement agencies receive grant funding to purchase equipment, administer training, and fund law enforcement and technical and administrative personnel to investigate and identify the locations of clandestine drug laboratories and conduct law enforcement actions to apprehend suspects and remove illegal drugs and other evidence. Grant-funded personnel may include, but are not limited to, sworn law enforcement personnel, analytical laboratory chemists, computer programmers, analysts, administrative staff, and specialized staff to administer specific methamphetamine initiatives, including but not limited to Drug Endangered Children and Small Rural Community programs. The DOJ COPS Office may also provide supplemental grants to previously funded agencies under the supplemental funding program.

Grant-funded equipment may include, but is not limited to, vehicles; surveillance equipment; health and safety equipment including personal protective equipment, environmental monitoring equipment, personnel decontamination equipment, and chemical analytical laboratory equipment and supplies, computer equipment (hardware and software), and office supplies. Grant funding may also be applied to administration of law enforcement, health and safety training, and other training.

After law enforcement actions are completed at a clandestine drug laboratory site, the site generally contains hazardous materials that were used in the production of illegal drugs, articles and fixtures that are contaminated with drug residues or hazardous materials, and/or drugs and drug precursors. Illicit production of methamphetamine may involve hazardous materials that are toxic, corrosive, flammable, or explosive. Such materials include anhydrous ammonia, sulfuric acid, hydrochloric acid, red phosphorous, lithium metal, sodium metal, iodine, and toluene. Upon discovery, the hazardous materials contained at clandestine drug laboratory locations are classified and managed as hazardous wastes. Under the DOJ COPS Methamphetamine Initiative grant award criteria and in accordance with Resource Conservation and Recovery Act (RCRA) regulations, the grantee becomes the legal "generator" of any hazardous waste that is identified in the conduct of grant-funded activities. Removal of the hazardous wastes from the discovered site therefore becomes the responsibility of the state or local law enforcement agency that discovers the materials. The state or local law enforcement agencies may either perform the removal action themselves using qualified law enforcement personnel or other qualified government personnel (referred to throughout this document as "qualified law enforcement personnel); Drug Enforcement Administration (DEA) hazardous waste management contractors; or other qualified contractors. State and local law enforcement agencies may also use grant funding to pay commercial hazardous waste disposal fees. The entity performing the hazardous waste removal action may package and transport the hazardous waste from the discovered clandestine laboratory to a temporary storage location. They also may repackage the hazardous wastes and/or consolidate the hazardous wastes into larger containers for transport, and then transport the hazardous wastes from the temporary storage unit to a permitted hazardous waste treatment and disposal facility. Under the Proposed Action, any hazardous waste management activity associated with clandestine laboratory seizures may be grant funded including hazardous waste removal, transportation, and storage, and payment of hazardous waste disposal fees. Grantees may theoretically be any non-Federal law enforcement agency. The DOJ COPS Office receives funding for the Methamphetamine Initiative from the Congressional annual appropriations cycle. Congress appropriates both "discretionary" and "earmarked" monies to the DOJ COPS Office Methamphetamine Initiative. Earmarked funds are designated for specific state and local law enforcement agencies and locations and are identified explicitly in the Federal budget appropriation language for the DOJ. Discretionary funds make up any remaining funding provided to the DOJ COPS Office, after earmarked funds are dispersed. All earmarked and discretionary grantees must comply with DOJ COPS Office Methamphetamine Initiative grant award conditions. The earmarked and discretionary grants for fiscal years 2001 and 2002 are presented in Appendix A and Appendix B respectively. The DOJ COPS Office Methamphetamine Initiative special grant award conditions are presented in Appendix C, Conditions of Grant Award; Appendix D, Special Condition for Methamphetamine Initiative: Mitigation of Health, Safety, and Environmental Risks and in Appendix E; Certification of Clean up of Clandestine Drug Laboratories. These conditions include meeting Federal, state, and local environmental laws and regulations. Environmental regulations that apply to grant-funded activities are discussed in Chapter 5.

The Proposed Action is the Current DOJ COPS Office Methamphetamine Initiative as described above. The only proposed alternative is the "No Action" Alternative, which is required to be assessed in accordance with Federal NEPA regulations. The No Action Alternative assumes that no Federal funding is provided to the DOJ COPS Office for the Methamphetamine Initiative and that no grant funding is awarded to prospective grantees. Under the No Action Alternative, state and local law enforcement entities would either have to find alternative funding for the activities for which grant funding is requested, or forego conducting such activities. The No Action Alternative assumes that no grant-funded clandestine drug laboratory seizures or other grant-funded activities are conducted. The Federally-funded DOJ COPS Office Methamphetamine Initiative and the proposed No Action Alternative constitute a major Federal action that is subject to the National Environmental Policy Act (NEPA) codified at 42 U.S.C. 4321, *et seq.* This Environmental Assessment was prepared in accordance with NEPA.

2.0   Purpose and Need for Proposed Action

2.1   *Purpose of Proposed Action*

The purpose of the Proposed Action is to implement the existing DOJ COPS Office Methamphetamine Initiative to provide grant funding to state, local, Tribal, and other public (not Federal) law enforcement entities to address clandestine methamphetamine laboratories and illicit methamphetamine use in their local and surrounding jurisdictions. Law enforcement agencies may apply grant funding to investigate and identify the locations of clandestine drug laboratories and conduct law enforcement actions to apprehend suspects and remove illegal drugs and other evidence, and equip and administer other programs related to methamphetamine, including Drug Endangered Children and Small Rural Community programs. The DOJ COPS Office may also provide supplemental grant funding to previously funded agencies. Grant-funded activities are classified for the purposes of this environmental assessment as hazardous waste management activities and other grant-funded activities. Grant-funded hazardous waste management activities may include removal of hazardous waste from seized clandestine drug laboratories (i.e., the removal action,) transportation and storage of such hazardous wastes, and the subsequent transport of such wastes to hazardous waste treatment and disposal facilities for disposal[1].

2.2   Need for Proposed Action

The Proposed Action is needed to supplement state and local methamphetamine initiative budgets because they cannot meet the entire burden of state and local-level clandestine drug laboratory initiative activities that are needed to combat the illicit production and distribution of methamphetamine. The incidence of clandestine drug laboratories has grown dramatically in the past 10 years. For example, in Fiscal Year 1992, the DEA's National Clandestine Laboratory Cleanup Program funded approximately 400 removal actions and by fiscal year 2001, the DEA Program funded more than 6,400 removal actions. The DOJ COPS Office has also found that the number of grant-funded seizures has increased sharply in recent years. The DOJ COPS Office anticipates that there may be a similar increase in the number of clandestine drug laboratory seizures conducted by state methamphetamine initiatives.

Grant-funded activities may include funding of personnel and overtime for sworn law enforcement officers and investigative, technical and administrative personnel, and funding for administration of law enforcement and health and safety training, and administration of Drug Endangered Children and Small Rural Community programs. Grant-funded activities may include community outreach and chemical and drug diversion investigation programs. Grants may be used to purchase law enforcement equipment including surveillance equipment, environmental monitoring equipment, personal protective equipment and other safety equipment used in clandestine drug laboratory seizures and hazardous waste removal actions, vehicles used to transport law enforcement personnel, law enforcement and safety equipment, evidence, or hazardous waste; chemical analytical laboratory equipment and supplies; and administrative and office supplies. A review of recent grant applications indicates that grantees use the funding for equipment and activities that they would otherwise not be able to fund themselves, and the funding enabled grantees to conduct more effective law enforcement activities, locate and seize clandestine drug laboratories, and reduce illicit production and use of methamphetamine. Clandestine drug laboratory seizure operations present unique hazards to law enforcement

---

[1] The term "removal" encompasses the characterization, packaging, labeling, marking, and physical removal of the hazardous wastes from the clandestine drug laboratory location.

personnel and the public. Hazardous materials contained at clandestine drug laboratory locations include drugs, drug precursors, other raw materials used for and byproducts of the manufacture of illegal drugs. These materials are toxic, corrosive, flammable, and/or explosive. According to statistics provided by the El Paso Intelligence Center (EPIC) NCLSS Reports, the DEA has estimated that 5 pounds of hazardous waste may be generated for every one pound of methamphetamine produced in a clandestine drug laboratory. These materials present health and safety hazards to law enforcement personnel entering the situation. Upon discovery of a clandestine laboratory, hazardous materials and booby traps pose health and safety hazards to the personnel performing the seizure and removal action. Availability of grant-funded personal protective equipment and other safety equipment has enabled law enforcement personnel to conduct seizures and removal actions safely. After seizure of suspects and evidence, hazardous materials left at a laboratory would pose a health and safety hazard to residents and the environment. In addition, the materials could be diverted and reused for illegal drug manufacture or other illicit purposes. Transporting and storing hazardous waste may also pose a hazard to the environment and human health and safety if not conducted properly. Grant funding has improved the capability and effectiveness of law enforcement agencies to conduct these activities.

2.3 Limitations of the Proposed Action

The environmental consequences analysis in the Environmental Assessment is limited to grant-funded activities. The DOJ COPS Office Methamphetamine Initiative does not provide funding for every aspect of state and local methamphetamine initiatives. The list of fiscal year 2002 Unallowable Costs and fiscal year 2002 Allowable Costs for the DOJ COPS Office Methamphetamine Initiative are provided in Appendix F and Appendix G. The DOJ COPS Office Methamphetamine Initiative will not fund salaries for existing personnel, but will fund overtime for existing personnel and salaries and benefits for new hire personnel. Funding for training is limited to topics that are directly linked to the Methamphetamine Initiative, such as health and safety training.

The term "removal action," for the purposes of this document, refers to the removal of bottles, cans, jugs, and other containers of hazardous waste and also to the removal of contaminated apparatus (e.g., glassware) and inextricably contaminated articles from a clandestine drug laboratory location. The DOJ COPS Office does not fund, and the Proposed Action does not include, further "cleanup" (i.e., environmental remediation) of residual hazardous wastes that may remain at clandestine drug laboratory sites after the removal action is completed. The term "environmental remediation," for the purposes of this document, refers to the cleanup of residual hazardous wastes that may remain in contaminated structures, soil, or water systems after the removal action is completed. The property owner, state or local health department, or state and local environmental agency would address any residual contamination that may remain at the site after removal actions are completed.[2]

---

[2] Based on the State and local governments that were contacted, law enforcement agencies typically notify the property owner concerning discovery of clandestine drug laboratories and the potential need for environmental remediation to be conducted after the removal action is completed. However, depending on

The Proposed Action also does not include any physical construction or modification of buildings or structures that would require site-specific environmental review under NEPA. In the event that any grant-funded construction or modification of buildings or structures is proposed, the DOJ COPS Office and/or the prospective grantee would conduct site-specific environmental review in accordance with Federal NEPA regulations and state environmental review regulations. Any proposed grant-funded construction or modification of buildings and structures is outside of the scope of this Environmental Assessment.

3.0   Summary of Impacts of the Alternatives

The Proposed Action evaluated in this Environmental Assessment include:

1) Continue the DOJ COPS Office Methamphetamine Initiative under which state and local agencies receive grant funding to investigate and seize clandestine drug laboratories and conduct related activities for their methamphetamine initiatives. This Alternative is referred to as the DOJ COPS Office Methamphetamine Initiative;

2) Discontinue the DOJ COPS Office Methamphetamine Initiative. Under this Alternative, the DOJ COPS Office would not receive federal funding for the Methamphetamine Initiative. In the event that the DOJ COPS Office does not receive Federal funding for the Methamphetamine Initiative, prospective grantees would be responsible for finding alternative funding to fund requested activities or forgo activities for which the grant funding was requested. This Alternative is referred to as the No Action Alternative.

The CEQ NEPA regulations require a comparison of the potential impacts of each Alternative. Table 3.0-1 summarizes the impacts for each Alternative across each of the impact areas.

---

the state or local jurisdiction, there may or may not be regulations requiring agencies to notify the property owner. Neither the DOJ COPS Office nor state or local law enforcement authorities are responsible for remediating residual contamination that may remain at the location after the removal action is completed. Similarly, there are not necessarily any regulations requiring a property owner to remediate a clandestine drug laboratory found inside a private residence. Some individual municipalities have passed laws allowing a law enforcement agency to recover costs from property owners after remediation.

Table 3.0-1 Summary of Impacts of Alternatives

	No Action Alternative[3]	DOJ COPS Office Methamphetamine Initiative[4]
Air Quality		
Clandestine Drug Laboratory Seizures	No grant-funded seizures or removal actions would be conducted under the No Action Alternative. Clandestine drug laboratories that are not seized because of resource limitations and continue to operate would represent a continuing source of illicit drug production and air releases. Hazardous waste remaining in place would result in ongoing and future air releases as a result of fugitive emissions from containers and contaminated articles and fixtures.	Grant funded clandestine drug laboratory seizures would reduce sources of illicit drug manufacture and air emissions. Air emissions from the normal conduct of clandestine drug laboratory seizures and associated hazardous waste removal actions are anticipated to be minimal.
Accidental Releases	No grant-funded removal actions would be conducted under the No Action Alternative. The potential for release of hazardous waste remaining in place is high. Releases could result from catastrophic release from or intentional breach of containers. Release of 100 kg of ammonia would result in an indoor concentration of 160,000 to 320,000 parts per million, resulting in fatality for persons exposed. Concentrations of ammonia in an adjacent apartment would be 6,400 ppm, resulting in severe health effects to exposed persons and impaired ability to take protective action. Concentrations in houses 50 feet from the point of release would equal the ERPG-2 of 150 ppm. Exposed persons would experience health effects, but not irreversible or other serious health effects or symptoms that would impair their ability to take protective action.	Releases of hazardous waste could result from breach of containers during removal action. However, the potential for such releases is much lower than if the hazardous waste were to remain in place. Release of 100 kg of ammonia would result in an indoor concentration of 160,000 to 320,000 parts per million, resulting in potential fatality for persons exposed unless personal protective equipment or rescue operations were employed. Concentrations of ammonia in an adjacent apartment would be 6,400 ppm, resulting in severe health effects to exposed persons and impaired ability to take protective action. Concentrations in houses 50 feet from the point of release would equal the ERPG-2 of 150 ppm. Exposed persons would experience health effects, but not irreversible or other serious health effects or symptoms that would impair their ability to take protective action.

---

[3] The No Action Alternative is based on the assumption that no grant-funded activities are conducted, and that the elimination of the Methamphetamine Initiative funding results in a reduction in the number of clandestine drug laboratory seizures as compared to the DOJ COPS Office Methamphetamine Initiative. Under the No Action Alternative, DEA contractors would cease conducting hazardous waste removal actions, and no grant funded hazardous waste transportation or storage activities would be conducted.

[4] The DOJ COPS Office Methamphetamine Initiative is based on the assumption that hazardous waste removal activities and transportation and storage activities associated with grant funded clandestine drug laboratory seizures would be conducted by qualified law enforcement personnel or other government personnel, DEA contractors, or other qualified grant-funded contractors.

Normal Operations Hazardous Waste Transportation and Storage	No grant-funded hazardous waste transportation or storage activities would be conducted under the No Action Alternative.	Fugitive air emissions from hazardous waste stored in storage units would be negligible under normal operations, assuming that the hazardous wastes are handled, packaged, transported and stored in accordance with regulatory requirements and grant award conditions. Vehicle emissions from hazardous waste transportation and other vehicle operations associated with grant-funded activities would be minimal as compared to overall agency vehicle operations.
Accidental Releases Hazardous Waste Transportation and Storage	No grant-funded hazardous waste transportation or storage activities would be conducted under the No Action Alternative.	Releases could result from transportation or materials handling accident at a storage unit. Release of 100 kg of ammonia from a transportation accident would result in a concentration of 150 ppm in houses 75 feet from the point of release. Exposed persons would experience health effects, but not irreversible or other serious health effects or impaired ability to take protective action. A release from an indoor storage unit would result in an indoor concentration of 80,000 ppm. Building occupants would suffer health effects unless they had personal protective equipment. Concentrations in houses 50 feet from the storage unit would exceed the ERPG-2. Exposed persons would experience health effects, but not irreversible or other serious health effects or impaired ability to take protective action.
Water Quality		
Clandestine Drug Laboratory Seizures	Clandestine drug laboratories that are not seized because of resource limitations and continue to operate would represent a continuing source of illicit drug production and releases to surface water. Hazardous waste remaining in place would result in ongoing and future releases of hazardous waste to surface water as a result of releases from containers. Such releases could contribute to exceedances of water quality standards and aquatic toxicity criteria, and result in exposure to hazardous wastes in surface water.	Grant funded clandestine drug laboratory seizures would reduce potential sources of releases to surface water. Surface water discharges from the normal conduct of clandestine drug laboratory seizures and associated removal actions are anticipated to be minimal, assuming that the hazardous wastes are handled, packaged, transported and stored in accordance with regulatory requirements and grant award conditions.

Accidental Releases Hazardous Waste Transportation and Storage	No grant-funded hazardous waste transportation or storage activities would be conducted under the No Action Alternative.	Release of hazardous waste to surface water could result from transportation or materials handling accident at a storage unit. The potential for such release may be higher for activities conducted by qualified law enforcement personnel than by DEA or other qualified contractors. Surface water quality and aquatic toxicity criteria could be exceeded in rivers or streams in the event of an uncontrolled 100-kilogram release of toluene or iodine to surface water. Releases from transportation accidents would be remediated by personnel conducting the transportation activity in accordance with regulatory requirements, minimizing the consequences of any release.
Accidental Releases Hazardous waste Transportation and Storage	No grant-funded hazardous waste transportation or storage activities would be conducted under the No Action Alternative.	Vehicles operated by qualified law enforcement personnel or other qualified contractors would not necessarily be placarded and hazardous waste manifests would not necessarily be prepared. Some grantees may be exempt due to Conditionally Exempt Small Quantity Generator's (CESQG) low-quantity exemption. DEA contractors are required to comply with RCRA SQG regulations for use of vehicle placards, manifests, and container markings, which could improve the timeliness of the response to a transportation accident release. Potential consequences for such release may therefore be higher for transport conducted by qualified law enforcement personnel or other qualified contractors than by DEA contractors.
Normal Operations Hazardous Waste Storage	No grant-funded hazardous waste transportation or storage activities would be conducted under the No Action Alternative	Releases to surface water from hazardous waste stored in storage units would be minimal, assuming that the hazardous wastes are handled, packaged, transported and stored in accordance with regulatory requirements and grant award conditions.
Soil Quality		
Clandestine Drug Laboratory Seizures	Clandestine drug laboratories that are not seized because of resource limitations and continue to operate would represent a continuing source of illicit drug production and releases to surface soils. Hazardous waste remaining in place would result in ongoing and future releases of hazardous waste to surface soils as a result of releases from containers. Such releases could contribute to exceedances of soil quality criteria, and result in exposure to hazardous wastes in surface soils.	Grant funded clandestine drug laboratory seizures would reduce potential sources of releases to surface soils. Releases to surface soils from the normal conduct of clandestine drug laboratory seizures and associated removal actions are anticipated to be minimal.

Normal Operations Hazardous Waste Storage	No grant-funded hazardous waste transportation or storage activities would be conducted under the No Action Alternative	Releases to surface soils from hazardous waste stored in storage units would be negligible, assuming that the hazardous wastes are handled, packaged, transported and stored in accordance with regulatory requirements and grant award conditions.
Accidental Releases Hazardous Waste Transportation and Storage	No grant-funded hazardous waste transportation or storage activities would be conducted under the No Action Alternative	Release of hazardous waste to surface soils could result from a transportation accident or a materials handling accident at a storage unit. The potential for such release may be higher for activities conducted by qualified law enforcement personnel than by DEA or other qualified contractors. Release of 100 kg of toluene or acetone to surface soils could exceed the generic soil screening level (SSL) concentrations levels for human ingestion of contaminated soils. Releases from transportation or materials handling accidents would be remediated by personnel conducting the activity in accordance with regulatory requirements, minimizing the consequences of any release.
Human Health and Safety		
Clandestine Drug Laboratory Seizures	Clandestine drug laboratories that are not seized because of resource limitations and continue to operate would represent a continuing source of illicit drug production and hazards to occupants of the clandestine drug laboratories and neighboring persons. Hazardous waste remaining in place would result in ongoing and future releases of hazardous waste to air, water, and soils as a result of fugitive releases from containers. Long-term exposure to releases could result in chronic health effects	Grant funded clandestine drug laboratory seizures would reduce health and safety hazards associated with the seized laboratories. The potential for health and safety impacts due to normal conduct of clandestine drug laboratory seizures and associated removal actions would be minimized given adherence with regulatory requirements and grant award conditions and through application of grant funded law enforcement and safety equipment and administration of grant funded health and safety training.
Normal Operations Hazardous Waste Removal Actions	No grant-funded hazardous waste removal actions would be conducted under the No Action Alternative	There is some potential for occupational exposure to hazardous wastes from removal actions, however such exposure would be minimized through training of qualified law enforcement personnel or qualified contractors conducting these activities. Occupational training provided to DEA contractors exceeds regulatory requirements for CESQGs. Qualified law enforcement personnel conducting removal actions would generally operate as CESQGs and receive only the training required for CESQGs. The potential for occupational exposure may therefore be higher for activities conducted by qualified law enforcement personnel than by DEA or other qualified contractors.

Normal Operations Hazardous Waste Transportation and Storage	No grant-funded hazardous waste transportation or storage activities would be conducted under the No Action Alternative	Public health and safety impacts would be negligible for normal operation of the storage units, assuming that the hazardous wastes are handled, packaged, transported and stored in accordance with regulatory requirements. The potential for releases and occupational exposure to such releases may be lower for activities conducted by DEA contractors and other qualified contractors than for similar activities conducted by qualified law enforcement personnel. Qualified law enforcement personnel may conduct such activities less frequently than DEA contractors and then only as required for the grant-funded initiative. The lower frequency of conduct of activities for law enforcement personnel may increase the potential for releases and occupational exposure.
Accidental Releases Hazardous Waste Transportation	No grant-funded hazardous waste transportation or storage activities would be conducted under the No Action Alternative.	Vehicles operated by qualified law enforcement personnel would not necessarily be placarded and manifests and container markings would not necessarily be prepared. Some grantees would be exempt due to CESQG's low-quantity exemption. The potential consequences of such releases may be higher for transport conducted by qualified law enforcement personnel than by DEA contractors. In the event that an unplacarded vehicle is involved in an accident or that hazardous wastes are released into the vehicle (e.g., through container seal failure), the driver and any passengers could be injured or disabled by the release. Such accident and resulting release could endanger response workers who do not know that the accident or release involves hazardous waste, and could also affect response time, as responders may not be able to determine what substances the occupants of the vehicle have been exposed to.
Other Grant Funded Activities	Under the No Action Alternative, no grant-funded activities would be conducted. Established grant-funded initiatives, including initiatives related to theft and diversion of anhydrous ammonia and other raw materials for methamphetamine production, would not be conducted, and no new initiatives would be established.	Grant funded initiatives, including initiatives related to theft and diversion of anhydrous ammonia and other raw materials for methamphetamine production, would reduce the production of methamphetamine and reduce health and safety hazards related to theft and mishandling of anhydrous ammonia and other methamphetamine raw materials.

Other Grant-Funded Activities	Elimination of availability of grant-funded law enforcement and safety equipment and administration of grant funded health and safety training may increase the potential for health and safety impacts, including occupational exposure, during clandestine drug laboratory seizure and associated hazardous waste management operations.	Application of grant-funded law enforcement and safety equipment and administration of grant funded health and safety training would reduce the potential for health and safety impacts, including occupational exposure, during clandestine drug laboratory seizure and associated hazardous waste management operations.
Social Effects		
Hazardous Waste Storage	No grant-funded hazardous waste transportation or storage activities would be conducted under the No Action Alternative.	The potential for diversion of hazardous wastes from storage units, and associated social effects of such a diversion, could be somewhat lower for transfer stations operated by DEA contractors (that require RCRA and SQG regulation) than for other storage units operated under this Alternative that meet regulatory requirements and grant award conditions. Although it is not anticipated that grant program personnel would present a risk of diversion, the locations where storage units may be situated (e.g., police stations, fire stations) could be accessible by non-program persons, including non-government personnel and members of the public, which could increase the risk of diversion. DEA's site security requirements for DEA contractors exceed RCRA regulatory requirements. Site security at transfer stations operated by qualified law enforcement personnel or other qualified contractors would meet, but not exceed RCRA regulatory requirements. Because DEA contractors would exceed RCRA and SQG regulations, the DOJ COPS Office anticipates that site security implemented at transfer stations by DEA contractors may be more stringent than site security implemented at other storage units operated under this Alternative, in particular with respect to outdoor storage units.

Impacts to Children	A significant potential for disproportionate impacts to children exists for the No Action Alternative. Clandestine drug laboratories that are not seized and continue to operate would represent a potential exposure pathway for children. Hazardous wastes are assumed to remain unattended and unsecured in either indoor locations or outdoor locations. In either case these unattended hazardous wastes, or contaminated soil resulting from release of such wastes, would represent a potential exposure pathway for children. Also, grant-funded Drug Endangered Children programs that have been established by grantees may not continue in operation, and no new grant-funded programs would be established.	Grant-funded clandestine drug laboratory seizures would reduce potential exposure pathways for children. Grant-funded Drug Endangered Children programs have been established by grantees that provide medial monitoring and child protection services for children found in clandestine drug laboratory sites.
Irreversible and Irretrievable Commitment of Resources	Under the No Action Alternative, no grant-funded activities would be conducted and no grant resources would be consumed.	Under the DOJ COPS Office Methamphetamine Initiative, resources would be expended in conducting grant-funded activities, including but not limited to the purchase of equipment, supplies, and consumables.
Environmental Justice	The No Action Alternative raises potential environmental justice concerns with respect to potential for disproportionate high and adverse impacts on minority and low-income populations. Laboratories may be located disproportionately in areas of minority or low-income population. Laboratories that not seized and hazardous waste remaining in place may disproportionately impact such populations.	The DOJ COPS Office Methamphetamine Initiative does not raise potential environmental justice concerns.
Energy Impacts	Under the No Action Alternative, no grant-funded activities would be conducted and no energy would be consumed conducting grant-funded activities.	Energy consumption for grant-funded activities would be insignificant as compared to the total amount of energy consumed by participating state and local government agencies as a whole.
Coastal Zone Management Act and Coastal Barrier Resources	Clandestine drug laboratories that are not seized may represent a continued potential impact to coastal zone resources.	Hazardous waste removal actions would result in reduction of potential for hazardous waste release to surface water and associated water quality impacts and ecological impacts to Coastal Zone Management Areas or Coastal Barrier Areas.
Historic Preservation	Clandestine drug laboratories are unlikely to be found in properties listed under or eligible for listing on the National Register of Historic Places. Therefore, the DOJ COPS Office does not anticipate impacts related to historic preservation.	Clandestine drug laboratories are unlikely to be found in properties listed under or eligible for listing on the National Register of Historic Places. Therefore, the DOJ COPS Office does not anticipate impacts related to historic preservation.

Wild and Scenic Rivers	Continued operation of clandestine drug laboratories and hazardous waste remaining in place would result in ongoing and potential future hazardous waste releases to surface water and associated water quality impacts and ecological impacts for any laboratories in the vicinity of a Wild and Scenic River.	Hazardous waste removal actions would result in reduction of potential for hazardous waste release to surface water and associated water quality impacts and ecological impacts to Wild and Scenic Rivers.
Threatened and Endangered Species	Continued operation of clandestine drug laboratories and hazardous waste remaining in place would result in ongoing and potential future hazardous waste releases to air, water, and soils and associated ecological impacts for any laboratories in the vicinity of a threatened and endangered species habitat.	Hazardous waste removal actions would result in reduction of potential for hazardous waste releases to air, water, and soils, and associated ecological impacts to any threatened and endangered species habitat.
Floodplain Management and Protection of Wetlands	The No Action Alternative would not result in any conversion of floodplains or wetlands. Continued operation of clandestine drug laboratories and hazardous waste remaining in place would result in ongoing and potential future releases to surface water and associated water quality impacts and ecological impacts for any laboratories in the vicinity of a wetland.	The Proposed Action would not result in any conversion of floodplains or wetlands. Hazardous waste removal actions would result in reduction of potential for hazardous waste release to wetlands and associated water quality impacts and ecological impacts.
Farmland Protection	The No Action Alternative would not result in any conversion of farmland.	The Proposed Action would not result in any conversion of farmland.

4.0   Description of Alternatives

This section describes the two Alternatives: the DOJ COPS Office Methamphetamine Initiative and the No Action Alternative.

4.1   DOJ COPS Office Methamphetamine Initiative

This alternative assumes the continued funding and implementation of the DOJ COPS Office Methamphetamine Initiative without any changes to the program. Under this alternative, Congress would continue to fund the DOJ COPS Office Methamphetamine Initiative. Since fiscal year 1998, the Methamphetamine Initiative has provided approximately $223 million to state and local agencies to fund personnel, purchase equipment, administer training, establish and administer special programs, and manage hazardous wastes recovered from clandestine drug laboratories. Congress funds the Methamphetamine Initiative through the annual appropriations process for "earmarked" and "discretionary" projects at state or local agencies. Earmarked projects and their funding levels appear explicitly in the Federal budget appropriation for the DOJ. Discretionary funds make up the rest of the total Federal funding provide to the DOJ COPS Office Methamphetamine Initiative. The DOJ COPS Office is aware that the ratio of earmarked to discretionary funding changes each year; some fiscal years there may be no discretionary funds. Total funding for fiscal year 2002 was $70 million.

The DOJ COPS Office assumes that grant funding would be requested for similar types of activities from one year to the next, and has based the environmental consequence analyses in this Environmental Assessment on discretionary and earmarked funding and grant applications for fiscal years 2001, 2002, and 2003. However, the DOJ COPS Office cannot predict what prospective grantees will request grant funding for in future years, or what earmarked funds may appear in Congressional budget authorizations in future years. The DOJ COPS Office anticipates that the activities identified in this Environmental Assessment and the associated environmental consequence analyses will bound the environmental impacts of future grant-funded activities.

Under the Proposed Action the DOJ COPS Office would continue to solicit applications for discretionary grants. The DOJ COPS Office reviews and approves applications and then issues an "award package" for the grantee to sign. Conditions of Grant Award and Special Condition for Methamphetamine Initiative: Mitigation of Health, Safety, and Environmental Risks in Appendix C and D respectively. Both earmarked and discretionary grantees are required as a condition of the grant award to comply with Federal, State, and local environmental, health, and safety laws and regulations applicable to their grant-funded activities, including activities relate to the investigation and seizure of clandestine methamphetamine laboratories and the removal, storage, transportation, and disposal of the chemicals, equipment, and solid and hazardous wastes recovered from or resulting from seizure of these laboratories. Appendix E, Certification of Cleanup of Clandestine Drug Laboratories, explains the requirements for removal actions performed at clandestine drug laboratories.
Grantees may use grant funding to perform their own removal actions and associated

hazardous waste transportation and storage using qualified law enforcement or other qualified government personnel, or use grant funding to hire qualified contractors to remove hazardous wastes from clandestine drug laboratory sites and subsequently transport, store, and dispose of the removed hazardous wastes. Grantees may also use DEA or state-funded contractors whose services are provided to state and local agencies. Non-grant funded hazardous waste management activities conducted for grant-funded clandestine drug laboratory seizures are not included as part of the Proposed Action.

The DOJ COPS Office Methamphetamine Initiative has in the past funded the purchase of hazardous waste transportation vehicles using earmarked funding and is anticipated to continue to fund the purchase, maintenance, and operation of hazardous waste transportation vehicles in the future. Therefore, the transportation of hazardous waste recovered from clandestine methamphetamine laboratories is included in the Proposed Action. Transportation includes conveying the hazardous waste from the clandestine drug laboratory location to a hazardous waste storage unit location and subsequently conveying the hazardous waste to a disposal facility, typically a treatment, storage and disposal facility (TSDF) as defined under the Resource Conservation and Recovery Act (RCRA). In most states, hazardous waste must not remain at the storage unit for more than 10 days if the storage unit is to be classified under RCRA as a "transfer station." If hazardous waste were stored at a storage unit location for more than 10 days, the storage unit would require a RCRA hazardous waste storage permit. Transfer stations used by licensed transporters to store hazardous waste for less than 10 days are covered under the hazardous waste transporter's license and are not required to be permitted under RCRA.

The DOJ COPS Office Methamphetamine Initiative also may also fund the purchase of hazardous waste storage units to be used as transfer stations. Grant funding may be used by some grantees to fund commercial hazardous waste facility disposal fees and therefore hazardous waste transportation, storage, and disposal are considered to be part of the Proposed Action.

The DOJ COPS Office also funds law enforcement and health and safety training of law enforcement personnel, salaries and benefits of sworn law enforcement personnel and civilians. Grant-funded law enforcement activities include surveillance and investigation, apprehension of suspects, seizure of clandestine laboratories, and collection and processing of evidence. Grants also fund the purchase of supplies and equipment. Appendix H shows the general types of equipment, supplies and training requested by grantees.

4.2   *No Action Alternative*

The No Action Alternative assumes loss of Federal funding and termination of the DOJ COPS Office Methamphetamine Initiative. Under the No Action Alternative, state and local law enforcement agencies that request funding for specific line items in their methamphetamine initiative budgets would be responsible for finding alternative funding for requested activities or forgoing conduct of such activities. Grantees are aware that funding is provided by Congress for the DOJ COPS Office Methamphetamine Initiative by Congressional appropriation, and that in the event that Congress does not appropriate funding no grant money would be dispersed to prospective grantees. The DOJ COPS Office recognizes that in some cases grantees may reprogram non-grant funding to enable them to conduct activities for which they requested grant funding, but this would not be possible for all activities for which grantees requested funding. The DOJ COPS Office Grant Award Conditions require that grant funding not be used to supplant existing funding. The DOJ COPS Office does not anticipate that prospective grantees would be able to replace a significant portion of the funding that would be eliminated if the No Action Alternative were implemented.

5.0 Hazardous Waste Removal, Transportation, and Storage Requirements

Hazardous materials discovered at clandestine drug laboratory locations may be classified as hazardous waste and may be required to be managed as hazardous waste. Removal actions require the management of hazardous waste, which is regulated under RCRA Subtitle C (42 USC 6901 *et seq.*). Grantees that use DOJ COPS Office Methamphetamine Initiative monies to perform removal actions at clandestine drug laboratory sites become classified as the legal "generator" of the hazardous waste recovered from the sites for the purposes of Federal, state, and local hazardous waste management requirements. Grantees performing their own removal actions or hiring contractors to conduct removal actions are required by the DOJ COPS Office to comply with the provisions of the RCRA regulations for hazardous waste generators (40 CFR 261 and 40 CFR 262) and related state and local hazardous waste management regulations. RCRA regulatory requirements are discussed in detail in Section 5.1.

DEA's requirements for DEA contractors exceed RCRA regulatory requirements. The DEA requires its hazardous waste management contractors to manage all hazardous materials recovered from clandestine drug laboratories as hazardous waste, regardless of whether the specific material is classified as a hazardous waste, and requires its contractors to dispose of such wastes in RCRA permitted TSDFs. This exceeds the minimum requirement set forth in RCRA. Qualified law enforcement personnel and other qualified contractors are required to meet federal, state and local regulations. The DOJ COPS Office does not require grantees conducting removal actions to manage all wastes removed from the sites as hazardous waste, and such wastes may be segregated from and managed separately from non-hazardous wastes recovered from the laboratory sites. The DOJ COPS Office requires grantees to meet federal state and local regulations and therefore it does not require that hazardous wastes generated from removal actions be disposed of at RCRA-permitted TSDFs. Certain states allow hazardous wastes generated by Conditionally Exempt Small Quantity Generators (CESQG) to be disposed of at non RCRA-permitted (generally state-permitted) disposal facilities.

Grantees that use DOJ COPS Office funding to purchase and operate vehicles to convey hazardous wastes from clandestine laboratory sites to a hazardous waste storage unit at another location are subject to hazardous waste transportation regulations. Transportation of hazardous waste is regulated by both the U.S. Environmental Protection Agency (EPA), under 40 CFR 263, and the U.S. Department of Transportation (DOT), under 49 CFR 171-179. Unless exempt from such requirements as a CESQG under RCRA, a transporter of hazardous waste must obtain an EPA identification number, comply with the hazardous waste manifest system to track hazardous waste shipments, and properly handle any hazardous waste discharges that may occur. Hazardous waste transportation regulatory requirements are discussed in Section 5.2

Under RCRA Subtitle C, a transporter of hazardous waste may store the waste for up to ten days at a transfer station. If hazardous waste were stored for more than ten days, the facility would be classified as a storage facility and would be subject to regulatory requirements for RCRA Treatment, Storage, and Disposal Facilities (TSDFs), which include RCRA permitting. The requirements for RCRA-permitted TSDFs (40 CFR 264-265) include general facility design and operating standards, standards for the various types of units in which hazardous waste is stored and managed, and personnel training. Grantees storing any quantity of hazardous waste for any length of time in a storage unit must meet certain National Fire Prevention Authority (NFPA) codes for storage of combustible and flammable materials. NFPA Codes have been codified as state regulations in 34 states. Regulatory requirements for hazardous waste storage and for combustible and flammable materials storage are discussed in Section 5.3.

5.1 RCRA Requirements

The responsibilities of any particular hazardous waste generator facility are based on the amount of hazardous waste being generated in any one calendar month. EPA Publication *Protocol for Conducting Environmental Compliance Audits for Hazardous Waste Generators under RCRA* (EPA 2001) summarizes federal regulations for hazardous waste generators[5]. Under federal regulations there are three classifications of hazardous waste generators:

Conditionally Exempt Small Quantity Generator (CESQG): A CESQG generates no more than 100 kg (220.46 lb.) of hazardous waste or no more than 1 kg (2.20 lb.) of acutely hazardous waste in a calendar month.[6] Under the provisions of 40 CFR 261.5, *Special Requirements for Hazardous Waste Generated by Conditionally Exempt Small Quantity Generators*, CESQGs are not subject to RCRA requirements for hazardous waste generators under 40 CFR 262 and are not subject to RCRA requirements for hazardous waste transportation under 40 CFR 263.[7] CESQGs may not accumulate on-site more than

---

[5] EPA 2001. *Protocol for Conducting Environmental Compliance Audits for Hazardous Waste Generators under RCRA*. United States Environmental Protection Agency, Enforcement and Compliance Assurance (2224-A), EPA 305-B-01-003, June 2001.

[6] None of the more than 7,500 clandestine drug laboratory removal actions for which hazardous waste quantity data were reported through EPIC in 2000, 2001, and 2002 involved the removal of wastes listed as acutely hazardous under RCRA.

[7] Note that certain state and local regulations differ from Federal RCRA regulations applicable to CESQGs. The State of Rhode Island does not recognize federal exemptions for small quantity generators, and the small quantity generator provisions of 40 CFR 261.5 do not apply in Rhode Island (RIR #DEM OWM-HW09-01, Rule 5.0.) The State of Kansas defines a "Kansas Generator" as generating 25 kilograms (55 pounds) or

1,000 kg (2,204.62 lb.) of hazardous waste at any one time. In the event that either the amount of hazardous waste generated in one calendar month exceeds 100 kg (220.46 lb.) or more than 1,000 kg (2,204.62 lb.) of hazardous waste have accumulated on-site, the facility is required to comply with the more stringent standards applicable to Small Quantity Generators (SQG). In the event that the amount of acutely hazardous waste generated in a calendar month exceeds 1 kg or the amount of waste generated from the cleanup of acutely hazardous waste exceeds 100 kg, then the waste is subject to standards applicable to large quantity generators (LQGs).

Small Quantity Generator (SQG): A SQG generates between 100 kg (220.46 lb.) and 1,000 kg (2,204.62 lb.) of hazardous waste in a calendar month. An SQG cannot accumulate hazardous waste on-site for more than 180 days unless the waste is transported more than 200 miles (321.87 km) to a treatment, storage and disposal facility (TSDF), in which case the hazardous waste may accumulate for up to 270 days. At no time may there be more than 6,000 kg (13,227.73 lb.) of hazardous waste accumulated at the facility. In the event that the amount of hazardous waste generated in a calendar month exceeds 1,000 kg (2,204.62 lb.) of non-acutely hazardous waste or 1 kg (2.20 lb.) of acutely hazardous waste, or the accumulation time limit is exceeded, the facility is required to comply with the standards applicable to LQGs. In the event that more than 6,000 kg (13,227.73 lbs) of hazardous waste is stored on-site, a SQG is required to obtain a RCRA hazardous waste storage permit and comply with the requirements applicable to hazardous waste storage facilities.

Large Quantity Generator (LQG): A LQG generates more than 1,000 kg (2,204.62 lb.) of hazardous waste or more than 1 kg (2.20 lb.) of acutely hazardous waste in a calendar month.[8]

Table 5.1-1 compares elements of the RCRA hazardous waste generator regulations applicable to CESQGs, SQGs, and LQGs.[9]

---

more and less than 1,000 kilograms (2,200 pounds) of hazardous waste in any calendar month (KAR Article 31 §28-31-2(d)). The federal regulatory threshold for a CESQG is 100 kilograms in any calendar month. The State of Arkansas requires CESQGs to manifest hazardous waste and transport the waste via a transporter permitted by the State of Arkansas (A.C.A. §§ 8-7-301, Regulation 23, §§ 262.35, 262.13).

[8] Water weighs approximately 8.34 lbs./gal (3.78 kg/gal or 1 kg/L). Using water as a basis of measurement, 100 kg (220.46 lb.) would equal about 26.4 gallons (100 L), or almost one-half of a 55-gallon (208.2 L) drum; 1,000 kg (2,204.62 lb.) would equal about 264 gallons (1000 L), or almost five 55-gallon drums.

[9] EPA 2001. *Protocol for Conducting Environmental Compliance Audits for Hazardous Waste Generators under RCRA.* United States Environmental Protection Agency, Enforcement and Compliance Assurance (2224-A), EPA 305-B-01-003, June 2001.

Table 5.1-1

Comparison of Elements of Federal RCRA Hazardous Waste Generator Requirements for CESQGs, SQGs, and LQGs

Requirement	CESQG	SQG	LQG
Calendar Month Hazardous Waste Generation Limit	<100 kilograms/month (<220.46 lbs/month)	100 - 1,000 kilograms / month	>1,000 kilograms / month (>2,204.6 lbs./month)
Calendar Month Acutely Hazardous Waste Generation Limit	<1 kg	-	>1 kg
On site Accumulation Limit	1,000 kilograms	6,000 kilograms	No Limit
Accumulation Time Limit	None.	180 days, or 270 days if waste is transported more than 200 miles to disposal	90 days, unless the facility obtains a RCRA storage facility permit.
RCRA Personnel Training Required?	No.	Yes. SQG personnel are required to be thoroughly familiar with proper waste handling and emergency procedures. (40 CFR 262.34(d)(5)(iii).	Yes. LQG personnel are required to obtain RCRA training. (40 CFR 262.34(a)(4) and 40 CFR 265.16(a) to (c).
Container Requirements for Accumulated Hazardous Waste	None Applicable.	Containers used at SQGs must be compatible with the wastes stored in them. Handling of incompatible wastes must comply with safe handling practices (40 CFR 262.34(d)(2) and 40 CFR 265.172, 265.173, and 265.177)	Containers used at LQGs must be compatible with the wastes stored in them. Handling of incompatible wastes must comply with safe handling practices. (40 CFR 262.34(a)(1)(i) and 40 CFR 265.172, 265.173, and 265.177)
Facility Design Requirements?	No.	SQG storage areas must be designed, constructed, maintained, and operated to minimize possibility of a fire, explosion, or unplanned release. (40 CFR 34(d)(4) and 40 CFR 265.30 to 265.37)	LQG storage areas must be designed, constructed, maintained, and operated to minimize possibility of a fire, explosion, or unplanned release. (40 CFR 34(a)(4) and 40 CFR 265.30 to 265.37)
Container Design Requirements?	No.	No.	Containers > ~26 gallons used at LQGs must meet design standards. (40 CFR 262.34 (a)(1)(i), 265,178, 265.1087(a) through (b)(1)(i) and (c))
Use Of Hazardous Waste Manifests Required for Transportation?	No.	Yes. (40 CFR 262.20, 262.42(b), and 262.44)	Yes. (40 CFR 262.20, 262.40, and 262.42(a))

Requirement	CESQG	SQG	LQG
DOT Hazardous Materials Transport Requirements applicable to Waste Transportation?	No.	Yes. (49 CFR 171.8 and 40 CFR 262.20, 262.42(b), and 262.44)	Yes. (49 CFR 171.8 and 40 CFR 262.20, 262.40, and 262.42(a))
"Self-Transportation" of waste by generator to another location allowed?	Yes.[10]	No. Licensed hazardous waste transporters must be used. (40 CFR 262.12(c))	No. Licensed hazardous waste transporters must be used. (40 CFR 262.12(c))
Emergency Response Coordinator Required?	No.	Yes. (40 CFR 262.34(d)(5))	Yes. (40 CFR 262.34(a)(4) and 40 CFR 265.55)
Inspection Required?	No.	Yes. Storage areas must be inspected each week. (40 CFR 262.34(d)(2) and 40 CFR 265.174)	Yes. Facility must have written Inspection Plan (40 CFR 262.34(a)(1)(i) and 40 CFR 265.178.)
Facility Contingency Plan Required?	No.	No.	Yes. (40 CFR 262.34(a)(4), 40 CFR 265.50 to 265.54)
Generator EPA Identification Number Required?	No.	Yes. (40 CFR 262.12(a) (b) and 40 CFR 265.11)	Yes. (40 CFR 262.12(a) (b))
Permitted or Interim Status Facilities must be used for waste disposal?	No.[11]	Yes. (40 CFR 262.12(c))	Yes. (40 CFR 262.12(c))
Maintain Waste Analyses, Tests and Determination records for 3 years since waste was sent to TSDF	No.	Yes. (40 CFR 262.40 (c)).	Yes. (40 CFR 262.40 (c)).
Storage Area Fire Prevention Design Requirements?	No.	Yes. (40 CFR 262.34(d)(4) and 40 CFR 265.3 – 265.37	Yes. (40 CFR 262.34(d)(4) and 40 CFR 265.3 – 265.37)

[10] Some States, including Arkansas, Minnesota and Wisconsin, require licensed transporters for CESQG waste.
[11] Some state regulations require disposal of CESQG waste in permitted disposal facilities.

Requirement	CESQG	SQG	LQG
Determine if Waste Requires Treatment Before Land Disposal (Restricted Waste)?	No.	Yes. (40 CFR 268.7(a)(1))	Yes. (40 CFR 268.7(a)(1))
Satellite Accumulation Points?	No.	Yes, as much as 55 gallons of hazardous waste or 1 qt. of acutely hazardous waste at or near initial point of generation. (40 CFR 262.34(c))	Yes, as much as 55 gallons of hazardous waste or 1 qt. of acutely hazardous waste at or near initial point of generation. (40 CFR 262.34(c))
Containment Building Operating Requirements?	No.	Yes.	Yes. (40 CFR 262.34(a)(1)(iv), 40 CFR 265.1101(a)(3), (c)(1), and (c)(4))
Packaging and Labeling Requirements for Off-site Transport (Complying with DOT Regulations)?	No.	No.	Yes. (40 CFR 262.30 through 262.33)
Ten-day storage limit at transfer facility in DOT approved containers?	Yes.	Yes. In the event that the ten-day limit is exceeded, the site would be classified as a hazardous waste storage facility subject to RCRA permit requirements.	Yes. (40 CFR 263.12)

This Page Intentionally Left Blank

State, local, and Tribal entities using grant funding to conduct hazardous waste removal actions would become classified as hazardous waste generators. Approximately 97 percent of hazardous waste removal actions reported by DEA in 2000, 2001, and 2002 involved less than 100 kilograms of hazardous waste, the threshold for classification as a CESQG. Occasionally, law enforcement agencies encounter more than 100 kilograms, or more than 1,000 kilograms, of hazardous waste to be removed from clandestine drug laboratories. DEA reported that 3 percent of removal actions involved more than 100 kilograms of hazardous waste and approximately 0.5 percent of removal actions involved more than 1,000 kilograms of hazardous waste.

The DOJ COPS Office Methamphetamine Initiative will not limit the quantity of hazardous waste that a grantee may handle in a single grant-funded removal action. If qualified personnel conduct removal actions involving more than 100 kilograms, or more than 1000 kilograms, of hazardous waste, the removal action would be subject to RCRA regulations for small quantity generators (SQG), or large quantity generators (LQG) respectively. The DOJ COPS Office will neither limit the period of time that hazardous waste may be stored in a hazardous waste storage unit. Therefore in some cases storage units may store hazardous waste for more than 10 days, and thereby require a RCRA permit to operate as a hazardous waste storage facility. It may also be the case that a grantee may accumulate more than 100 kilograms of hazardous waste at a temporary storage location, even if individual removal actions are limited to 100 kilograms or less (i.e., the grant-funded agency discovers more than one laboratory in the same week, or month.) However, some states (e.g., California, Nebraska) regulate the amount of hazardous waste that may be self-transported and limit the period of time that the waste could be stored in a storage unit.

According to statistics provided by the El Paso Intelligence Center (EPIC) NCLSS Reports from 2000, 2001, and 2002 (to date) the average amount of hazardous waste removed from clandestine drug laboratory sites is approximately 20 kilograms (44 pounds) of hazardous waste per site. A summary of the reported data for hazardous waste removal actions for 2000, 2001, and 2002 is included in Table 5.1-2. More than 50 percent of the 7,572 removal actions for which data were reported involved the removal of less than 3.5 kilograms (7.7 pounds) of hazardous waste, and more than 97 percent of the removal actions involved the removal of less than 100 kilograms (220 pounds) of hazardous waste. These data do not include all removal actions conducted by state or local law enforcement agencies, but only those removal actions reported to EPIC. The DOJ COPS Office anticipates that the characteristics of grant-funded removal actions would be similar to the characteristics of removal actions reported to EPIC.

The average amount of 20 kilograms of hazardous waste recovered at a clandestine drug laboratory location, and attributed to a single hazardous waste generator and generated within any calendar month, would be under the RCRA threshold for classification as a CESQG. As discussed above, the DOJ COPS Office Methamphetamine Initiative will not limit the quantity of hazardous waste removed, transported or stored by a grantee.

Table 5.1-2

Average Amount of Hazardous Waste Removed from
Clandestine Drug Laboratory Sites

Reporting Calendar Year	2000	2001	2002	Total/Average
Total all hazardous waste reported recovered (kg)	31,139.6	86,232.0	33,243.6	150,615.2
Total reported removal actions (Job Numbers)	1,896	3,554	2,122	7,572
Average quantity per Job Number (kg)	16.4	24.3	15.7	19.9
Job Numbers with quantity > 100 kilograms	47	124	60	231 (3.0%)
Job Numbers with quantity > 1000 kilograms	3	8	2	13 (0.2%)

Note: Data are reported for calendar years 2000 and 2001 and for January – August 2002
Source: El Paso Intelligence Center (EPIC) NCLSS Reports from 2000, 2001, and 2002 (to date)

Because the grantees become the legal generators of hazardous waste found and removed from clandestine methamphetamine laboratories, grantees would be responsible for meeting the requirements for the quantities of waste recovered, transported, and stored. The DOJ COPS Office anticipates that most agencies conducting removal actions would operate as CESQGs. However, in some cases grantees may operate as SQGs or LQGs, or operate a RCRA-permitted hazardous waste storage facility. Note that some state regulations limit the quantity of hazardous waste that may be removed, transported, or stored without a RCRA permit.[12] In the event that a grantee does not wish to obtain a RCRA permit for managing quantities of waste greater than 100 kilograms or greater than the threshold amount set by state regulations, (or any amount of acutely hazardous waste,) the grantee may contact a DEA contractor, or in some states a state-funded contractor (e.g., California), to conduct the removal action, and transport, store, and dispose of the hazardous waste. In either case the state and local law enforcement agency conducting clandestine drug laboratory seizures becomes the legal hazardous waste generator for any hazardous waste encountered at the laboratory location. In the event that Federal funding is not available for the conduct of removal actions (e.g., under the No Action Alternative) the state or local agency remains responsible for managing the hazardous wastes encountered.

Although most clandestine drug laboratory removal actions involve quantities of hazardous waste that would be classified under the CESQG threshold, the DEA National Clandestine Laboratory Cleanup Program (which may conduct grant-funded removal actions under the Proposed Action) is structured to meet the more stringent requirements applicable to SQGs, including training of hazardous waste management personnel and preparation of hazardous waste manifests. DEA contractors are required to implement additional security requirements for removal, transportation, and storage of the hazardous waste, and are required to classify all hazardous materials recovered from clandestine drug

---

[12] Some states limit the amount of hazardous waste that a CEQSG generator can transport without obtaining a hazardous waste transportation license. For example, the State of California restricts CEQSG generators to transporting 23 kilograms of hazardous waste. The State of Kansas limits CESQGs to generate no more than 20 kgs. of hazardous waste in a calendar month, while the federal RCRA threshold for CESQGs is 100 kgs.

laboratories as hazardous waste.

5.2 DOT Regulatory Requirements

In addition to RCRA requirements, the shipment of hazardous waste from clandestine laboratory sites to temporary storage units is also subject to DOT regulations for the transport of hazardous waste (49 CFR 171-179). DOT defines hazardous waste as any hazardous material for which RCRA provisions require a Hazardous Waste Manifest. Therefore the applicability of DOT regulations depends on the EPA's definition of hazardous waste under RCRA and on the exemptions from manifesting requirements as specified in RCRA. In particular, waste that qualifies for a CESQG exemption is not required to conform to DOT regulations for transport of hazardous waste.

The DOT regulations for the transport of hazardous waste include general provisions governing approved containers and packaging methods, labeling and marking of containers and packages, use of identification numbers to classify specific hazards, placarding of transport vehicles, use of shipping papers, incident reporting, emergency response information, training, and procedural requirements when using motor vehicles on public highways. The DOT general provisions and exemptions for limited quantities and small quantities are shown in Table 5.2-1 and described below.

General Provisions

Unless a hazard-specific quantity exemption is provided for, the DOT provisions prescribe rigorous design standards for the packages and containers that are used to transport all types of hazardous waste. Specific labels are required for all portable containers and non-bulk packages containing hazardous materials that are listed in the DOT Hazardous Materials Table (i.e., 49 CFR 172.101). Generators and transporters must mark each package, freight container, and transport vehicle containing hazardous waste with the shipping name, material identification number, technical names, and other information as specified in 49 CFR 172.300 *et seq.* For shipments of over 1,000 pounds (454 kilograms) of hazardous waste, placards specific to the relevant hazard class must be affixed to the transport vehicles. Hazardous waste shipments must be accompanied by readily accessible shipping papers that contain all relevant information needed to identify and safely handle the waste, and to respond appropriately in the event of an emergency.

The general provisions also require certain reporting measures in the event of a hazardous waste release. For example, transporters must contact the National Response Center in the case of a major incident. To help reduce the probability of an incident, Hazmat employees must receive training in materials identification, safety, accident prevention, emergency response measures, and issues specific to the mode of transport in which they are engaged. For example, the regulations require certain loading, unloading and materials segregation procedures when motor vehicles are used to transport hazardous waste on public highways.

Table 5.2-1

Federal DOT Requirements for the Transport of Hazardous Waste[13,14]

Requirement	General[15]	Limited Quantities	Small Quantities
Packaging	Specific approved packages and containers are required for each type of hazardous material, as specified in Section 173. Methods of packing and storage that affect transport safety must be open to inspection.	Up to 30 kg (gross weight) of certain hazardous materials (e.g., oxidizers and corrosives) are exempted from these DOT-specification packaging requirements when placed in combination packages in conformance with hazard-specific requirements.[16,17]	Up to one ounce of certain hazardous liquids, solids and compressed gases are exempted from these specific packaging requirements.[18] Packages must conform to the broad guidelines provided in 49 CFR 173.4.
Labeling requirements	Specific labels are required for all portable containers and non-bulk packages that contain hazardous materials listed in the Hazardous Materials Table.[19]	Not required.	Not required. (See 49 CFR 172.400a)

[13] CESQGs are not required under RCRA regulations to transport hazardous wastes in accordance with EPA and DOT regulations. DEA contractors are required to comply with RCRA regulations for SQGs, including utilization of hazardous waste manifests, container markings, and vehicle placards, regardless of the quantity transported. The DOJ COPS Office does not anticipate that vehicles used to transport hazardous wastes generated from CESQGs would be equipped with DOT-regulation placards or that hazardous wastes being transported would be accompanied by manifests, unless required by state regulation.

[14] Iodine, an solid oxidizer and a corrosive that has been found in large quantities at clandestine drug laboratories, does not appear to be regulated by DOT and is therefore not subject to DOT packaging or transportation regulations. This may represent a potential environmental hazard with respect to the Proposed Action because iodine is incompatible with and reacts with, among other hazardous materials, ammonia, which has also been found in large quantities at clandestine drug laboratories.

[15] Applies to each person who transports (or offers for transport), a hazardous material that is not otherwise exempted.

[16] See, for example, 49 CFR 173.152 and 49 CFR 173.154 for limited quantity specifications for oxidizers and corrosives, respectively. Combination packages are large packages that contain smaller, separate units of specified capacity, with intermediate packaging.

[17] State hazardous materials transportation regulations also regulate packaging of hazardous materials, including anhydrous ammonia. For example, Illinois Public Act 91-0889 prohibits transport of anhydrous ammonia in a portable container if the container is not a package authorized for anhydrous ammonia transportation as defined in rules adopted under the Illinois Hazardous Materials Transportation Act. Other states, including Washington, have similar laws.

[18] These quantities are far lower than the quantities of hazardous waste to which the CESQG exemption applies. Therefore materials in these quantities are also exempt from DOT regulations for the transport of hazardous waste under RCRA regulations. See 49 CFR 173.4 and 173.306.

[19] See 49 CFR 172.101 and 49 CFR 172.411 through 172.450

Requirement	General[15]	Limited Quantities	Small Quantities
Marking requirements	Generators and transporters must mark each container and transport vehicle containing a hazardous material according to specifications in 49 CFR 172.300 et seq.[20] (including shipping name, material identification number, and technical names).	Same as general unless specified otherwise below (e.g., specific exemptions for identification numbers).	Packages must be marked as follows: "This package conforms to 49 CFR 173.4"
Identification numbers	The DOT ID number of each hazardous material must be marked on its packaging. (See 49 CFR 172.334)	Not required.	Not required.
Placarding of Vehicles	Hazard-specific placards must be affixed to vehicles used to transport hazardous waste.	Placards are not required when the transported waste consists of less than 1000lbs (454kg) of certain hazardous materials.[21]	Not required. These general requirements also do not apply to non-bulk packaging that contains only residue of certain materials.[22]
Shipping papers	Hazardous waste must be accompanied by shipping papers that identify and describe the waste, hazard class, ID number, packaging group, capacity, emergency contact information, and signed certification from the waste generator.[23]	Same as general. Limited quantity materials must also be identified as such on the shipping papers.[24]	Not required.
Reporting	In the case of an incident while transport is underway, the driver must contact the carrier.[25] In the case of a major incident, transporters must contact National Response Center.	Same as general.	Not required.
Required Emergency Response Information	The shipping paper must contain the name and description of the material, immediate hazards to health, risks of fire or explosion, immediate actions to be taken, first aid information, and the telephone number of someone to provide comprehensive emergency response information.[26]	Same as general.	Not required.

[20] As specified in 49 CFR 172.300
[21] See 49 CFR 172.504. The pertinent wastes include all of those typically found at clandestine laboratories, e.g. flammable and non-flammable liquids, flammable and non-flammable gases, flammable solids, oxidizers and corrosives.
[22] These include several classes of explosives, as well as flammable gas, non-flammable gas, poison gas, flammable liquid, flammable solid, spontaneously combustible materials, oxidizers, and corrosives. Together these exemptions comprise all the types of materials that have been found in significant quantities at clandestine drug laboratories by the DEA over the past three years.
[23] See 49 CFR 172.204
[24] See 49 CFR 172.500.
[25] See 49 CFR 172.606
[26] See 49 CFR 172.602.

Requirement	General[15]	Limited Quantities	Small Quantities
Availability of Emergency Response Information	Must be immediately accessible at all times to hazmat employees, including drivers, at any facility where a hazardous material is received, stored or handled during transportation, and any government employee responding to or investigating an incident.[27]	Same as general.	Not Applicable.
Hazardous Waste Manifests	Waste shipments must be accompanied by manifests developed jointly by EPA and DOT for this purpose. Manifests may replace shipping papers.	Not required based on CESQG exemption in RCRA regulations. State regulations may require use of hazardous waste manifests for transport of CESQG hazardous waste.	Not Applicable.
Hazardous Materials Training Requirements	Hazmat employers[28] must ensure that hazmat employees[29] are trained in material identification, safety, accident prevention, and emergency response.[30] States may require more stringent requirements. OSHA/EPA training may be used to avoid duplication. In addition, carriers must ensure that drivers receive modal-specific training.[31]	Same as general.	Not Applicable.
Use of Motor Vehicles and Public Highways	Procedures for loading/unloading hazardous materials into/from a motor vehicle for highway travel must adhere to requirements particular to each type of material.[32] In addition, during loading/unloading, intermediate storage and transport, materials must be segregated according to specified safety standards.[33]	Same as general.	Not Applicable.

[27] 49 CFR 172.600, 172.602 and 49 CFR 172.604
[28] Includes any private or public sector individual who uses employees to help transport hazardous materials.
[29] Includes any private or public sector employee, including a driver, who directly affects hazardous materials transportation safety.
[30] 49 CFR 172.700 and 49 CFR 172.702
[31] This includes training specific to the transport of hazardous materials by motor vehicle as well as standard motor vehicle operation training as specified in 49 CFR parts 390 through 397.
[32] 49 CFR 173.30 and 49 CFR 177.834 and 49 CFR 177.835 through 177.841.
[33] 49 CFR 177.848

Limited Quantities

Up to 30 kg of certain hazardous materials (e.g., oxidizers and corrosives) qualify for a limited quantity exemption from the general packaging specifications, provided they are packed according to certain guidelines in containers that meet a list of performance standards. These guidelines and standards require the sub-packaging of wastes in small quantities (e.g., 1 liter of liquid), which may be placed together with other units in combination packages in conformance with hazard-specific requirements. Limited quantity shipments under this exemption are not required to follow the labeling requirements, and are not required to use material-specific identification numbers.

Generators and transporters of limited quantities must follow the marking requirements specified in the general provisions, or may use a special exemption marking if the broad packaging guidelines contained in 49 CFR 173.13 are used. Placards are not required on vehicles transporting limited quantities of hazardous waste. Shipments of limited quantities must, however, be accompanied by shipping papers, which must additionally specify that the shipment contains hazardous wastes transported as a limited quantity. Finally, limited quantity shipments must conform to the general provisions for reporting release incidents, HAZMAT employee training, and procedures specific to the use of motor vehicles for the transport of hazardous waste on public highways.

Small Quantities

Certain very small quantities of specific hazardous wastes are exempted from all DOT general provisions, as long as they are packaged according to the broad guidelines provided in 49 CFR 173.4, and marked with a label stating this to be the case. The allowable small quantities are 1 ounce for both liquid and solid wastes that belong to certain waste classes, e.g. corrosives, oxidizers, and flammable liquids and solids.

DOT Regulations and the CESQG Exemption Under RCRA

As discussed above, waste generators are not required under RCRA to use a hazardous waste manifest for the transport of CESQG wastes. The required use of the hazardous waste manifest determines the applicability of DOT regulations for the transport of hazardous waste. Since virtually all of the grant-funded removal actions are expected to involve the removal of less than 100 kilograms (220 pounds) of hazardous waste, the DOJ COPS Office expects nearly all grant-funded removal actions to be carried out using the CESQG exemption. Hence the DOT regulations for the transport of hazardous waste would not apply to the vast majority of removal actions.

5.3 Fire Protection Codes

Fire protection codes and regulations are applicable to the storage of hazardous wastes at storage units under the Proposed Action. Grantees must consider the National Fire Protection Association (NFPA) Code 30, Flammable and Combustible Liquids Code, and

NFPA Code 230, Standard for Fire Protection of Storage when storing hazardous wastes removed from clandestine methamphetamine drug laboratories.[34][35] The NFPA Code 30 has been adopted as statewide fire protection regulations in 34 states, including Arkansas, Iowa, Kansas, Louisiana, Missouri, Nebraska, New Mexico, North Dakota, Texas, Utah, and all states east of the Mississippi River except Indiana and Pennsylvania.[36] The hazardous materials found in clandestine methamphetamine laboratories may be classified as flammable, combustible, toxic, reactive, caustic, and as incompatible with other materials. For example, NFPA Code 30 divides liquids by properties and classes. Flammable liquids, known as Class I liquids, are defined as having a flash point less than 100 degrees F. Combustible liquids are known as Class II liquids and are defined as a liquid having a flash point of 100 degrees F or higher.

For flammable and combustible liquids, many of the NFPA Codes for storage of have been adopted in OSHA Regulation 29 CFR 1910.106, Occupational Safety and Health Standards: Flammables and Combustible Liquids.[37] RCRA regulations also address fire protection requirements for the generation, transportation, and storage of hazardous wastes. Grantees storing hazardous waste for more than a 10 day period are required to obtain a RCRA hazardous waste storage facility permit and must meet RCRA requirements for hazardous waste storage, including safety and fire protection standards. NFPA Codes and OSHA regulations also apply to permitted hazardous waste storage. These regulations are intended to prevent unauthorized persons from physical contact with the waste or equipment and are intended to prevent ignition or reaction of ignitable or reactive waste. Warning signs are obligatory, as are emergency communication equipment, firefighting equipment, and water or foam supplies. Grantees must provide space for movement of personnel and fire/spill control equipment. In the event of a spill, the operator of a RCRA permitted facility must be able to contain any flow and clean up any release of hazardous wastes. Regulations for Storage of Flammable and Combustible Materials are summarized in Table 5.3-1.

---

[34] NFPA, 2000. National Fire Protection Association, NFPA Code 30, Flammable and Combustible Liquids Code, 2000 Edition.
[35] NFPA, 1999. National Fire Protection Association, NFPA Code 230, Standard for Fire Protection of Storage, 1999 Edition.
[36] NFPA, 2002. Comprehensive Consensus Codes™ NFPA 30, Flammable and Combustible Liquids Code, http://www.nfpa.org/BuildingCode/aboutc3/nfpa_30/nfpa_30.asp
[37] OSHA requirements apply only to the storage of flammable or combustible liquids in drums or other containers (including flammable aerosols) not exceeding 60 gallons individual capacity and those portable tanks not exceeding 660 gallons individual capacity.

Table 5.3-1
Regulations for Storage of Flammable and Combustible Materials

Requirement	Description	Location
Container and Portable Tank Storage	Storage of flammable and combustible liquids in containers and design of storage units	29 CFR 1910.106(d)
Storage of flammable and combustive hazardous wastes	Types and quantities	NFPA Code 30 and 20 CFR 1910.106(d)
Fire protection requirements	Generation, transportation, and storage of hazardous wastes	40 CFR 262.34(d)(4), 264.14 - 264.37, and 265.3 to 265.37
Storage and handling of anhydrous ammonia	Storing anhydrous ammonia away from ignitable materials and fire hazards either in a separate building areas or section of the building	American National Standard for the Storage and Handling of Anhydrous Ammonia, K61.1, OSHA 1910.111
Storage cabinets for flammable liquids	Design, construction and capacity requirements	OSHA regulations, 29 CFR 1910.106(d)(3).

The DOJ COPS Office anticipates that grantees performing their own removal actions using qualified law enforcement personnel would store the hazardous waste in storage units either inside or outside a building. In either case, flammable liquids may be stored in a "storage cabinet" whereas flammable liquids and other hazardous materials may be stored in a hazardous materials "storage locker." Storage cabinets are usually indoor storage units. Storage lockers are prefabricated structures designed to meet local, state, and federal requirements for outside storage of hazardous materials. The lockers are primarily for outdoor storage, but may also be used inside a building.

Storage cabinets for flammable liquids must meet design, construction and capacity requirements. Storage cabinets may be constructed of metal or wood and must be designed and constructed to withstand certain fire tests. These flammable liquids storage cabinets are not required to have exhaust ventilation systems under NFPA Code 30. However, NFPA does indicate that most cabinets are designed to be equipped with such ventilation systems. Flammable liquids storage cabinets that are located indoors also do not need to be vented. However, if the cabinet is vented, it must be vented outside the building from the bottom with make-up air supplied from the top.

Safety regulations for storage of hazardous waste also limit the quantities of waste than may be stored in a cabinet or locker. For example, not more than 60 gallons (approximately 200 kilograms) of Class I or Class II flammable liquids and not more than 120 gallons of Class III liquids may be stored in a single storage cabinet according to OSHA. However, quantities above 200 kilograms of Class I or II flammable liquids would require multiple storage cabinets under OSHA.

Restrictions on quantities of flammable materials stored either inside or outside are dependent on "fire area" ratings. A "fire area" is defined as an area of a building separated by the rest of the building by some construction that has a fire resistance of at least one hour. All "communication openings" (e.g., doors) also must have the same fire resistance of at least one hour.[38] Both OSHA regulations (29 CFR 1910.106(d)(4)) and NFPA Code 30 allow up to approximately 1,000 kilograms (300 gallons) in one 150 square foot area with a one-hour fire resistance.

Indoor Storage

For indoor storage, NFPA Code 30 allows up to three 60-gallon storage cabinets in one fire area. Under OSHA and NFPA, any quantities above 1,000 kilograms and below 2,000 kilograms would require fire protection in the form of sprinkler, water spray, carbon dioxide or other system. Further, quantities above 2,000 kilograms would also require a 2-hour fire resistance for inside rooms. NFPA Code 30 provides requirements for automatic fire protection based on the type of container (e.g., metal, fiberboard, glass), and the type, quantity, and storage style (e.g., pile, rack) of the flammable liquid. According to OSHA, the inside storage room would have to have a gravity or mechanical exhaust ventilation system. Also, both OSHA regulations (29 CFR 1910.106(d)(5)) and NFPA Code 30 specify that Class I flammable liquids may not be stored in the basement of a building.

OSHA and RCRA regulations and NFPA Codes specify acceptable storage conditions and locations permitted for indoor storage of flammable materials. Storage cabinets are not to be located near exit doorways, stairways, or means of egress, and are not to be located near ignition sources. Indoor windows should be protected as specified in OSHA regulations and in NFPA Code 251-1969 Standard Methods of Fire Tests of Building Construction and Materials. Also, according to NFPA Codes for inside storage rooms, all electrical wiring must meet Class I, Division 2 requirements for Class I flammable liquid storage.

Outdoor Storage

If hazardous materials or flammable liquids are stored outside, they may be stored in hazardous materials lockers, piles, or pallets. However, they must meet a variety of OSHA regulations and NFPA Code 30 requirements including minimum distance to access way. Flammable liquids may be storage in piles of containers, but cannot exceed certain quantities. Examples of these quantities per pile are given in Table 5.3-2.

Table 5.3-2
Pile Size for Flammable Liquids

Flammable Liquids	Pile Size
Class IA	1,100 gallons
Class IB	2,200 gallons

---

[38] Resistance rates may be more than one hour depending on whether the room is an inside room, cutoff room, or liquid warehouse. Inside room is a room totally enclosed in a building without exterior walls; cutoff room has at least one exterior wall, and liquid warehouse is separate detached building for warehousing liquids.

Class IC	4,400 gallons

Source: NFPA Code 30 and OSHA

The smallest size pile is sufficiently more than 1,000 kilograms such that the DOJ COPS Office anticipates that only a single pile would be needed for most storage activities. Distances between piles and distances between the pile and the property line or street are also provided in NFPA Code 30 and OSHA. For example, according to OSHA, for Class IA liquids, the distance between a pile and a property line must be at least 20 feet and between a pile and a street or alley must be at least 10 feet. Further, there are requirements for the pile adjacent to a nearby building. The storage area must be graded to divert possible spills away from buildings to drain such spills in contained locations. The storage areas must be protected against tampering or trespassers.

In addition to flammable liquids, there may be toxic, reactive, caustic, and other types of hazardous materials found in clandestine methamphetamine laboratories. A range of toxic, explosive materials including flammables and combustibles liquids are included hazardous materials definitions in 40 CFR 1910 and OSHA. According to NFPA Codes, hazardous materials present hazards beyond the fire problems related to flash point and boiling point. The hazards may arise from a materials' toxicity, reactivity, instability, or corrosivity.

In accordance with NFPA Code 30, these toxic, reactive, unstable, and corrosive materials may be stored in hazardous materials storage lockers that may be placed inside or outside a building. If stored inside a building, the same limitations as described for storage cabinets apply. If stored outside a building, the lockers must meet regulatory requirements such that lockers shall not exceed 1,500 square feet of floor area. Lockers should have spill containment to prevent flow of liquids from the structure during an emergency and there should be appropriate distances between the lockers (e.g., five feet) and between the locker and the property line. Unpackaged materials (not in original packaging) should only be stored in shelves or on the floor of the locker. Containers over 30 gallons storing Class I or Class II liquids should not be stored more than two containers high. Additionally, all placarding or warning signs for lockers should be in accordance with all federal, state, and local regulatory requirements and in accordance with NFPA 704 Standard System for the Identification of the Hazards of Materials for Emergency Response.

It should be noted that both EPA and individual states (e.g., California) have regulations and guidelines related to storage of incompatible hazardous wastes (e.g., corrosive materials and flammable materials.)[39] Incompatible materials may be required to be stored in different cabinets, or to be separated by barriers if stored within the same cabinet. In that case, grantees may be required to have specially designed storage units that incorporate such barriers, or may be required to have more than one storage unit, in order to store the various types of hazardous waste that are anticipated to be recovered at clandestine drug laboratory sites, depending upon the specific types of hazardous wastes

---

[39] California Code of Regulations CCR Title 24, Part 8, Section 7902; California Fire Code, Section 8001.11.8.

recovered from removal actions.

5.4 DOJ COPS Office Methamphetamine Initiative Policies and Procedures

The DOJ COPS Office Methamphetamine Initiative Policies are outlined in the *Methamphetamine Initiative Grant Owner's Manual.* Grant conditions are established within the Public Safety Partnership and Community Policing Act of 1994, under which the COPS office was established. Other policies are applicable as issued by the DOJ, the Office of Management and Budget (OMB), the General Accounting Office, the US Treasury, the EPA, OSHA and DOT. Personnel who remove hazardous wastes and contaminated materials from a clandestine laboratory site must be "qualified" to do so. In order to be considered "qualified," an individual must comply with all Federal, State, and local environmental, health and safety laws and regulations applicable to the removal of all hazardous wastes and contaminated materials from a clandestine laboratories. These include, but are not limited to RCRA (40 CFR 260, et seq.,) OSHA regulations (29 CFR 1910.120 and Part 1200), and DOT regulations on the labeling and transportation of hazardous wastes (49 CFR 171, et seq. and Parts 350-399.)

The grant conditions establish policies to which grantees agree. Procurement requirements are addressed regarding competitive bids for contractors. Allowable costs are outlined with the intention to help policing agencies develop infrastructure to institutionalize and sustain policing practices. Allowable costs include but are not limited to salaries and benefits, overtime, training, travel, consultants, and equipment. It is the intention of the DOJ COPS Office to supplement, not supplant funds for activities that would not have take place in the absence of the grant.

The DOJ COPS Office seeks to document on a continuing basis the proper use of federal funds by grantees. The DOJ COPS Office conducts evaluations and requires periodic progress and quarterly financial status reports. Grantees must confirm that they are in compliance with federal audit requirements and OMB regulations. The reports must contain information on the status of funded activities, updates on hiring activities, updates on the purchase and installation of any grant-funded equipment and technology, and any progress the agency has made with respect to law enforcement as a result of its involvement in the Methamphetamine Initiative. The DOJ COPS Office requires that grantees operating inter-jurisdictional criminal intelligence systems (a system that receives, stores, analyzes and exchanges data regarding ongoing criminal activities) comply with operating principles in 28 CFR Part 23. Grantee activities may be further monitored through telephone calls and/or site visits from representatives of the DOJ COPS Office. In FY 2003, grantees will be required to file reports to the DOJ COPS Office. The report forms are currently being reviewed and approved by OMB. In FY 2003, grantees will also have to report clandestine drug laboratory seizure activities to EPIC and RiskNet.

Grantees must also agree to any special conditions as determined by the DOJ COPS Office. One such special condition is the Special Condition for Methamphetamine Initiative: Mitigation of Health, Safety, and Environmental Risks (Appendix D). The DOJ

COPS Office expects grantees to comply with all federal, state, and local environmental health, and safety laws and regulations during all aspects of grant funded activities. Specific federal regulations are discussed in Sections 5.1, 5.2 and 5.3 of this Environmental Assessment. Grantees are responsible for complying with any state and local regulations, which may be more stringent than some federal requirements.

6.0 Environmental Consequence Analysis Scenarios

6.1 Scope of Methamphetamine Initiative

The incidence of clandestine drug laboratories has grown dramatically in the past 10 years. For example, in Fiscal Year 1992, the DEA funded approximately 400 removal actions at clandestine drug laboratory locations. In fiscal year 2001, the DEA funded removal actions at more than 6,400 locations, and DEA anticipates funding approximately 7,255 removal actions in fiscal year 2002. Clandestine drug laboratories are still most prevalent in the West, Midwest, and Southwest, but are becoming more prevalent in the Southeast. There are at present relatively few clandestine drug laboratories discovered in the Northeast. More than 500 DEA-funded removal actions were conducted in Arkansas, Oklahoma, Tennessee, and Texas in fiscal year 2001, and between 200 and 500 DEA-funded removal actions were conducted in Alabama, Arizona, Colorado, Georgia, Illinois, Iowa, Minnesota, Mississippi, and Washington. These statistics do not include all clandestine drug laboratory seizures conducted by state methamphetamine initiatives. The DOJ COPS Office does not have comprehensive statistics concerning the number of grant-funded clandestine drug laboratory seizures conducted, however, the number of grant-funded seizures has increased sharply in recent years.

The increasing rates of removal actions and recent grant application project summaries indicate that states are dependent upon DOJ COPS Office Methamphetamine Initiative funding to support and supplement their methamphetamine initiatives. Several state initiatives have been receiving a significant amount of funding through the DOJ COPS Office Methamphetamine Initiative, and several states, including Missouri, have received funding for several initiatives operating in different geographic areas of the state. The state initiatives discussed in detail in Appendix I are California, Hawaii, Missouri, Washington, Iowa, Wisconsin, Arkansas and Mississippi.

6.2 Hazardous Waste Management Scenarios Development Approach

The environmental consequence analyses are based on analysis of scenarios for the two principal activities associated with the Proposed Action: grant-funded hazardous waste management activities at clandestine drug laboratory locations, and other grant-funded activities. Hazardous waste management activities include the seizure of laboratories, removal, transportation and the temporary storage of hazardous waste recovered from laboratory seizures. The scenario development methodology for the hazardous waste management scenarios focused on the types of clandestine drug laboratory structures and the types of neighborhoods in which the clandestine drug laboratories were discovered, and on the characteristics of the transportation equipment and storage units that may be used to the manage hazardous wastes recovered in the removal actions.

For the purposes of the quantitative environmental consequences analysis, the DOJ COPS Office assumed an accidental release scenario of 100 kilograms of hazardous waste. This release scenario was applied to the air, water and soil quality analyses. The quantitative analysis is based on a release quantity of 100 kilograms because an anticipated 97 percent of removal actions would involve less than 100 kilograms of hazardous waste, and because the DOJ COPS Office anticipates that for most grant-funded removal actions the largest single container of hazardous waste handled, transported, or stored would contain 100 kilograms. The DOJ COPS Office does not require grantees to restrict grant-funded removal actions to less than 100 kilograms quantity, and therefore Section 8.0 includes a qualitative discussion of handling, transportation, and storage of quantities of hazardous waste greater than 100 kilograms. For the qualitative analysis of the fire scenario the DOJ COPS Office assumed that more than 100 kilograms of flammable material may be stored at a single location and involved in the fire. Individual hazardous waste storage units may contain more than 100 kilograms of hazardous waste.

6.3   *Removal Action Scenario Development*

The removal action scenarios were developed to reflect the most common characteristics of clandestine drug laboratory locations. The DEA administers the National Clandestine Laboratory Cleanup Program, for which it maintains a database of clandestine drug laboratory seizures reported through the National Clandestine Laboratory Seizure System (NCLSS) at the El Paso Intelligence Center (EPIC). As of Fiscal Year 2003, grantees will be required to report seizure operations to EPIC and RiskNet, however, detailed data for state and locally conducted laboratory seizures for 2000, 2001, and 2002 are not available. In the absence of such data, DEA data were used. The reporting system characterizes clandestine drug laboratory seizures with respect to laboratory structure (e.g., single family house), laboratory neighborhood (e.g., urban), and the types and amounts of hazardous wastes seized at the location. The types and quantities of hazardous wastes discovered at clandestine drug laboratory locations vary depending on the types and quantities of illegal drugs being produced.

6.3.1   Clandestine Drug Laboratory Hazardous Waste Quantity Data

NCLSS data for clandestine drug laboratory hazardous waste removals for 2000, 2001, and 2002 are summarized in Table 6.3-1. Table 6.3-1 illustrates the hazardous wastes (chemical names) removed from clandestine drug laboratory sites and the number of sites where removal of that specific hazardous waste was reported. Relevant physical and chemical characteristics of these wastes are summarized in Appendix J, Health Hazards of Chemicals Used in Methamphetamine Production. Based on data for 2000, 2001, and 2002 (to date) the average amount of hazardous waste removed from clandestine drug laboratory sites was 20 kilograms (44 pounds), and 97 percent of removal actions for which data were reported involved removal of less than 100 kilograms of hazardous waste.

Table 6.3-1
Hazardous Wastes Recovered from DEA-funded
Removal Actions at Clandestine Drug Laboratory Sites

Chemical Name	Total quantity recovered from all sites (kg)			Maximum recovered from any site (kg)
	2000	2001	2002	
2,5-DIMETHOXYBENZALDEHYDE	340.69	0	0	340.69
ACETIC ANHYDRIDE	19.03	25.77	4.91	17.28
ACETONE	1,827.76	5,012.79	1,713.67	1,001.69
AMMONIA GAS (COMPRESSED)	5,842.27	26,447.38	12,510.18	2,305.04
ANTHRANILIC ACID	0	801.65	0.10	801.65
BUTYLAMINE	21.39	0	0	21.39
CYCLOHEXANONE	0	75.76	0.10	75.76
EPHEDRINE	265.41	1,238.33	215.56	429.68
ERGOMETRINE	0	1.5	0	1.50
ETHYL ACETATE	14.81	18.52	2.54	17.77
ETHYL ETHER	969.05	1,574.59	348.05	369.68
ETHYLAMINE	0	0	0.38	0.38
FORMAMIDE	0	2.27	0	2.27
FORMIC ACID	94.60	0	0	91.60
HYDRIODIC ACID	185.69	595.35	93.09	387.90
HYDROCHLORIC ACID	1,292.88	1,900.79	1,100.92	136.33
IODINE	4,337.46	17,068.34	10,756.72	1,732.22
IODINE (CRYSTALS)	4,898.43	2,718.41	1,571.45	1,866.21
LITHIUM METAL	2.25	210.59	44.54	28.30
METHAMPHETAMINE LIQUID	3.47	0.45	8.99	3.78
METHYL ETHYL KETONE	53.56	23.58	17.59	15.24
METHYLAMINE	20.58	19.63	0	17.07
N-ACETYLANTHRANILIC ACID	12.49	0.50	0	12.49
N-ETHYLEPHEDRINE	0	1.89	0.11	1.89
NITROETHANE	0.79	0	0	0.79
O-TOLUIDINE	0	0	0.05	0.05
PHENETHYLAMINE	0	2.40	28.35	28.35
PHENYL-2-PROPANONE(P2P)	0	0.96	0	0.96
PHENYLACETIC ACID	11.69	5.11	0	11.69
POTASSIUM PERMANGANATE	4,506.97	0.81	517.60	4,476.49
PSEUDOEPHEDRINE	5.93	52.13	12.15	28.35
RED PHOSPHORUS	1,858.23	20,619.61	855.56	6,930.45
SAFROLE	0	0	1.58	1.04
SODIUM DICHROMATE	1.19	2.50	1.02	2.50
SODIUM METAL	10.20	0.94	*0.45*	8.52
SULFURIC ACID	1,925.06	4,086.83	1,631.78	210.67
THIONYL CHLORIDE	0	40.90	0	15.43
TOLUENE	2,617.76	3,681.68	1,806.16	623.57

The specific hazardous wastes examined in the removal action and storage scenarios and release scenarios include the toxic and flammable chemicals that were found at clandestine drug laboratories. Data for removal actions are shown in Table 6.3-1. One of the most common hazardous wastes recovered is anhydrous ammonia. Thus, the quantitative analysis of environmental consequences related to air quality impacts for the removal action and storage scenarios focuses on the environmental effects of releases of 100 kilograms of ammonia. The quantitative analysis of potential impacts to soil quality is based on releases of acetone and toluene, and also on releases of sodium dichromate, which was included in the analysis based on the toxicity of the substance. The quantitative analysis of impacts to potential water quality is based on releases of toluene and iodine.

Based on historical data, DEA estimates that the number of clandestine drug laboratory seizures could increase by as much as 35 percent per year over the next five years. The DOJ COPS Office anticipates that there may be a similar increase in the number of clandestine drug laboratory seizures conducted by state methamphetamine initiatives. The environmental consequence analyses assume that the types and quantities of hazardous wastes that are recovered from each individual removal action will remain relatively constant for the next five years, but that the total number of sites and the total amount of hazardous wastes recovered from all sites will increase by 35 percent per year over the next five years.

6.3.2 Clandestine Drug Laboratory Site Characteristics Data

Clandestine drug laboratories have been discovered in diverse structures, including vehicles, single-family houses, hotel/motel rooms, apartments, condominiums, mobile homes, businesses, storage lockers, and in open space areas (*i.e.,* no structure). NCLSS data for clandestine drug laboratory structures for 2000, 2001, and 2002 are summarized in Table 6.3-2. Neighborhoods where clandestine drug laboratories have been discovered include commercial, industrial, rural, suburban, and urban locations. NCLSS data for 2000, 2001, and 2002 are summarized in Table 6.3-3. The DOJ COPS Office has assumed for the purposes of the environmental consequence analyses that characteristics would be similar to those reported by the DEA.

Table 6.3-2
Clandestine Drug Laboratory Site Characteristics – Laboratory Structure

Laboratory Structure	2000	2001	2002	TOTAL
Apartment	588	701	334	1623
Business	4	103	70	177
Condominium	28	34	11	73
Hotel/Motel	341	444	205	990
Mobile Home	847	1268	569	2684
Not Identified	270	496	617	1383
Open Air/No Structure	965	2531	1199	4695
Other	1256	1485	505	3246

Public Land	0	0	1	1
Single Family House	3356	4204	1745	9305
Storage Locker	158	177	64	399
Vehicle	1453	2035	1022	4510
TOTAL	9266	13478	6342	29086

Table 6.3-3
Clandestine Drug Laboratory Site Characteristics – Laboratory Neighborhood

Laboratory Neighborhood	2000	2001	2002	TOTAL
Commercial	379	461	282	1122
Industrial	156	174	79	409
Other	250	137	67	454
Public Land	0	0	11	11
Rural	3363	5833	2812	12008
Suburban	2367	3359	1043	6769
Urban	1847	2530	1141	5518
Unknown	914	1048	978	2940
TOTAL	9276	13542	6413	29231

Note: Data for 2002 include seizures reported for January–August 2002

The potential environmental consequences of hazardous waste removal actions may differ significantly based on the characteristics of the laboratory structure and neighborhood where the laboratory is discovered, as well as on the types and quantities of hazardous waste discovered. Because clandestine drug laboratory structures and neighborhoods are diverse, three generic scenarios have been developed for the environmental consequence analyses in this Environmental Assessment. These scenarios are anticipated to reflect the range of potential environmental consequences associated with the Proposed Action.

In developing the removal action scenarios, NCLSS Report data from 2000, 2001, and 2002 (to date) was used to characterize the types of clandestine drug laboratory structures and the types of neighborhoods where they were discovered. The data indicate that the major portion of the clandestine drug laboratories discovered in the past three years were located in rural, urban, or suburban neighborhoods, as opposed to commercial or industrial areas. The removal action scenarios for the Proposed Action are based on rural, urban, and suburban locations because of greater incidence of human and ecological receptors in those areas than in commercial or industrial areas.

Examination of the NCLSS data revealed that the four largest categories of structure types for clandestine drug laboratories are single-family houses, open air/no structure, mobile homes, and apartments. For the purposes of analyses, single-family homes and mobile homes are aggregated into a single category, *single-family house*, and apartments and condominiums are aggregated into a single category, *multi-unit residential property*. The open air/no structure category has characteristics that are significantly different than categories that involve structures. Therefore *open air/no structure* is considered a separate category for the environmental consequence analyses. Other clandestine drug laboratory structure categories (*i.e.,* hotel/motel, vehicle, storage locker, business) included in the NCLSS Reports are anticipated to have environmental settings and characteristics that are within the boundaries of the single-family house, multi-unit residential property, and open air/no structure categories. Therefore the environmental consequences analyses in this Environmental Assessment do not analyze all categories but focus on the most prevalent three categories.

However, the DOJ COPS Office cannot determine from the NCLSS data for example, the number of single-family houses reported and number of rural neighborhoods reported, or the number of single-family houses located in rural neighborhoods or the number of apartments located in urban neighborhoods. Therefore, the structure category and neighborhood category data were combined into three scenarios:

- Single Family House (Urban, Suburban, Rural)
- Multi-unit Residential Property (Urban, Suburban); and
- Open Air/No Structure (Rural)

The basis for these scenarios is that single family houses (including mobile homes) may occur in urban, suburban, or rural neighborhoods, while multi-unit residential properties (apartments, condominiums) are somewhat more likely to occur in urban and suburban neighborhoods than in rural neighborhoods. Open air/no structure clandestine drug laboratories are somewhat more likely to occur in rural neighborhoods. Also, for the purposes of the environmental consequences analyses, an open air/no structure clandestine drug laboratory located in a rural neighborhood would have potentially greater consequences with respect to ecological receptors than if located in an urban or suburban neighborhood. The scenarios used for the environmental consequences analyses are described in the following section.

Clandestine drug laboratories discovered by DEA and by state and local law enforcement authorities have contained booby traps. These are constructed by suspects to deter law enforcement authorities, and may be chemical, mechanical, or explosive in nature. Table 6.3-4 summarizes data from the NCLSS Reports concerning booby traps. Booby traps may be detected and disarmed by law enforcement authorities in the function of their law enforcement activities, however in some cases an undetected booby trap may remain at a clandestine drug laboratory site after law enforcement activities are completed.

Table 6.3-4
Clandestine Drug Laboratory Site Characteristics – Booby Traps Discovered

Booby Traps Discovered	2000	2001	2002	TOTAL
Chemical	20	9	1	30
Mechanical	3	1	2	6
Explosive	8	2	0	10
Type Not Identified	5	37	4	46
TOTAL	36	49	7	92

6.3.3   Single Family House Removal Action Scenario

The Single Family House Removal Action Scenario reflects the characteristics of clandestine drug laboratory locations that are reported in the NCLSS Reports as "Single Family House" in the *Laboratory Structure* category and reported as "Urban," or "Suburban," in the *Laboratory Neighborhood* category. This scenario is intended to reflect locations where the laboratory and hazardous wastes are located in a single family house where a release of hazardous wastes could contaminate the structure and/or soil, or result in exposure of residents, and where a hazardous waste fire, explosion, or booby trap could cause injury or ignite a structural fire.

In this scenario, a clandestine drug laboratory is situated in the basement and or ground floor of a wood-frame single-family house. The single-family house is assumed to be a two-story house with a basement and with bedrooms on the second floor. The house has a backyard and the backyard area may also have been used as a storage area for hazardous wastes. The house and backyard area are assumed to be adjacent to other single-family houses on three sides (the fourth side being the street) and the backyard is fenced. It is also assumed that neighboring single-family houses remain occupied by adults and children during conduct of removal actions.

6.3.4   Multi-unit Residential Property Removal Action Scenario

The Multi-unit Residential Property Scenario reflects the characteristics of clandestine drug laboratory locations that are reported in the NCLSS Report as "Apartment" or "Condominium" in the *Laboratory Structure* category and reported as "Urban," or "Suburban" in the *Laboratory Neighborhood* category. This scenario is intended to reflect locations where the clandestine drug laboratory and associated hazardous wastes are in a multi-unit dwelling and where a release could result in exposure of adjacent dwelling residents or where a hazardous waste fire, explosion or booby trap could cause injury to adjacent dwelling residents or ignite a structural fire that could affect adjacent dwelling units. The Multi-unit Residential Property Scenario represents a multi-unit dwelling in which a clandestine drug laboratory and associated hazardous wastes are situated in one dwelling unit of a multi-story, multi-unit dwelling. It is also assumed that neighboring dwelling units remain occupied by adults and children during conduct of removal actions.

6.3.5   Rural Open Air Setting Removal Action Scenario

The Rural Open Air Setting Scenario reflects the characteristics of clandestine drug laboratory locations that are reported in the NCLSS Report as "Open Air/No Structure" in the *Laboratory Structure* category and that are reported as "Rural" in the *Laboratory Neighborhood* category. This scenario is intended to reflect clandestine drug laboratory locations where hazardous wastes are not contained by any building or other permanent structure and are exposed to the elements, and where the clandestine drug laboratory is located in the vicinity of surface water, wetlands, vegetation and species habitat. A release of hazardous wastes in such an environmental setting could directly contaminate soil or surface water. A hazardous waste fire, explosion, or booby trap in such an environmental setting could ignite an outdoor fire. Unsecured hazardous waste containers could be relatively easily removed from the clandestine drug laboratory location and diverted to other locations, if not subject to removal action. It is assumed that suspects or other persons do not occupy the location, and that there are no residential or commercial structures in the vicinity. It is also assumed that the topography of the site is such that storm water runoff (and any entrained hazardous wastes) would flow towards a nearby surface water body including wetlands areas.

6.4   Transportation Scenarios

After removal from a clandestine drug laboratory, hazardous wastes would be packaged at the site into containers appropriate for hazardous waste transportation, and transported to storage locations, where the wastes would be stored temporarily prior to transportation to a permitted facility for treatment and disposal. Grantees may utilize qualified law enforcement personnel or other qualified government personnel to self-transport hazardous waste, or utilize DEA contractors or other qualified contractors to transport hazardous wastes generated from removal actions. Grantees would need to obtain a hazardous waste transporter license to self-transport waste that is not CESQG waste.[40]

6.4.1   Self-transport Scenario

The DOJ COPS Office anticipates that hazardous wastes that are self-transported by grantees would be transported in small to medium-sized trucks or trailers and would generally be transported in 5-gallon, 20-gallon, or 55-gallon containers. The DOJ COPS Office anticipates that for most removal actions the grantee transporting the hazardous waste would be operating as a CESQG (i.e., generating less than 100 kilograms of hazardous waste in a calendar month), and therefore the CESQG exemptions from RCRA and DOT regulations for hazardous waste shipments would apply.

According to DOJ COPS Office grant award criteria, grantee personnel who would be involved in the seizure or closure of clandestine laboratories must be equipped with OSHA-required personal protective equipment and safety equipment as appropriate for the site conditions, and receive OSHA initial health and safety and annual refresher training. The DOJ COPS Office award criteria require that grantees that conduct hazardous waste management activities receive training in accordance with RCRA regulatory requirements for hazardous waste generators. Due to the wide applicability of the CESQG exemption to grant-funded removal actions, the DOJ COPS Office anticipates that personnel conducting removal actions and hazardous waste transportation would receive only a limited amount of training in the management and transport of CESQG hazardous wastes. Specifically, the CESQG exemption allows the transport of less than 100 kilograms of CESQG waste to proceed without adherence to RCRA and DOT regulations pertaining to:

---

[40] It should also be noted that, while self-transport of CESQG wastes are permitted under RCRA, at least eleven States, including Arkansas and Wisconsin, require CESQG wastes to be transported by a licensed hazardous waste hauler, or require the CESQG to obtain a hazardous waste transport license to self transport the CESQG hazardous waste. Other states, including Missouri, allow CESQGs to self transport hazardous wastes without obtaining a hazardous waste transport license.

- Container design / packaging (RCRA/ DOT)
- RCRA Personnel Training and DOT Hazmat training[41]
- Hazardous waste manifest / shipping papers (RCRA/DOT)
- Containment building operating requirements (RCRA)
- Facility contingency plans (RCRA)
- Markings and labeling (DOT)
- Placarding of vehicles (DOT)
- Emergency response information (DOT)
- Procedures for loading/unloading into trucks traveling on highways (DOT)
- Segregation of incompatible materials (DOT)

DEA contractors are required to comply with RCRA and DOT regulatory requirements pertaining to SQGs, including regulations pertaining to utilization of hazardous waste manifests, hazardous waste container labels, and vehicle placards, regardless of the quantity transported. The DOJ COPS Office assumes that hazardous waste manifests, container labels, and vehicle placards would not be utilized in conduct of self-transport of CESQG waste, unless required by state regulation, and that self-transporters of CESQG waste would not comply with Federal RCRA and DOT regulations for which CESQGs are exempt, except if such Federal regulations are superceded by state regulations. The DOJ COPS Office also assumes that self transport of CESQG wastes would be conducted by grantees only on an as needed basis, and that grantees would not accumulate day to day experience in conducting hazardous waste transportation activities, as would a qualified commercial hazardous waste contractor. This would be the case even in states, such as Arkansas and Wisconsin, where CESQGs are required to obtain hazardous waste transport licenses to self- transport CESQG waste. RCRA regulations do not permit self-transport of hazardous waste that is not CESQG waste. Therefore, grantees that conduct removal actions that generate more than 100 kilograms of waste would be required to use qualified hazardous waste transporters or obtain transporter license themselves.

6.4.2   Licensed Transport Scenario

Grantees may not self-transport CESQG waste in certain states without obtaining a hazardous waste transport license, and non-CESQG hazardous waste cannot be self transported. Although the CESQG exemption from RCRA and DOT regulations for the transport of hazardous materials would apply to the licensed transport scenario, the DOJ COPS Office has assumed for the purposes of the environmental consequences analysis in the environmental assessment that in the event that a grantee chooses to, or is required to, transport CESQG waste using a licensed hazardous waste transporter, that the licensed transporter is likely to meet the requirements for the transport of larger amounts of hazardous waste. Some grantees (e.g., Arizona, Hawaii) have provided grant funding to DEA contractors to perform hazardous waste management activities that are outside the scope of the National Clandestine Laboratory Cleanup Program. DEA contractors are

---

[41] Certain states have their own requirements for the training of hazardous waste transporters.

required to comply with RCRA and DOT regulations applicable to SQGs concerning use of hazardous waste manifests, hazardous waste container markings, and vehicle placards.

The DOJ COPS Office assumes that licensed transporters of hazardous waste, including DEA contractors and other qualified contractors, would accumulate day-to-day experience with and knowledge of appropriate procedures for the safe handling and transport of hazardous materials. In addition, licensed hazardous waste transporters are subject to more extensive training requirements that pertain to transport of larger volumes of waste (e.g. SQG and LQG) and conduct of emergency response in the event of a transportation accident or other hazardous waste release. These factors may affect the timeliness and effectiveness of emergency response in the event of an incident.

6.5   *Storage Scenarios*

Under the Proposed Action, the DOJ COPS Office assumes that hazardous wastes recovered from clandestine drug laboratories would be stored temporarily in either indoor or outdoor storage units. The DOJ COPS Office has assumed for the purposes of the environmental consequences analysis that storage units would be located either indoors or outdoors at a police station or fire station. As noted above, the DOJ COPS Office has not restricted the quantity of hazardous waste that a grantee may temporarily store, provided that the grantee meets RCRA and DOT requirements and DOJ COPS Office grant award conditions. Specific locations of proposed future storage units cannot be anticipated. Therefore, the environmental consequence analyses for the transportation and storage scenarios are not location-specific.

The security measures at DEA contractor-owned and operated transfer stations exceed the requirements of Federal and state hazardous waste management regulations, and may therefore exceed security measures implemented at other storage unit locations. Qualified and trained DEA contractor personnel permanently staff the transfer stations and are subject to security investigation and clearances from the DEA. In terms of physical security, the transfer stations are surrounded by six foot, three strand barbed wire fences and generally have additional security measures such as video surveillance cameras. Hazardous wastes generated from clandestine drug laboratory removal actions are required to be segregated from other types of hazardous waste that are being managed at the DEA contractor transfer stations, and are stored in accordance with NFPA Code 30, NFPA Code 230 and other fire protection codes and building codes.

6.5.1   Indoor Storage Unit Scenario

Under the DOJ COPS Office Methamphetamine Initiative, storage units are anticipated to be situated at indoor locations in government-owned buildings (e.g., fire stations, police stations.) The DOJ COPS Office assumes that indoor storage units would be enclosed areas constructed inside an existing government-owned permanent structure, specifically for the purpose of storing hazardous waste recovered from clandestine drug laboratory sites. The DOJ COPS Office also assumes that other hazardous materials used at the facility (e.g., paint, solvents) would not be stored in the same enclosure or immediately adjacent to the enclosed area[42]. The DOJ COPS Office anticipates that the indoor enclosed area in which the storage unit is situated would be segregated and secured from other areas of the building by permanent fixtures (e.g., doors, gates) and that only authorized and qualified personnel would have access to the enclosed area. Indoor storage units would be equipped with spill containment and fire protection systems in accordance with grant award conditions and in accordance with fire protection and building codes. Fire protection codes applicable to indoor storage of flammable and hazardous materials are summarized in Section 5.3.

For indoor storage of flammable and hazardous materials (including hazardous wastes), the materials may be stored in a building that is not primarily used for chemical storage. The indoor storage unit may be situated in a corner of a large room or perhaps a separate room (and separate fire area) designed for chemical storage. A separate room may be needed for indoor storage of larger quantities of materials, such as greater than 1,000 kilograms (300 gallons). An inside storage room would have to have a mechanical or gravity exhaust ventilation system. The indoor storage scenario can be broken down into storage of flammables (e.g., class I and class II liquids) and the storage of hazardous materials (e.g., ammonia, acids). It is anticipated that small quantities of flammables would be stored in a storage cabinet that can store a maximum of 60 gallons (equivalent to more than 100 kilograms). Flammable liquids storage cabinets that are located indoors do not need to be vented, however, if venting is used, the unit must be vented to outside the building. If vented, the storage cabinet must be vented from the bottom with make-up air supplied from the top. Hazardous materials lockers would be used to store larger quantities of flammable and other hazardous materials.

For indoor storage of quantities of 100 kilograms or less of Class I flammable and hazardous materials, it is anticipated that at least two storage cabinets or at least two hazardous materials lockers would be sufficient. At least two storage units would be needed so that incompatible substances will not be commingled. The DOJ COPS Office assumes that the fire protection areas would be 200 square feet in area to accommodate the storage units. With this size fire protection area, the walls, ceiling, and floors would need the typical 1-hour fire resistance for this size rooms/fire area. No additional special fire protection such as sprinklers or water sprays would be needed other than those needed for the building in general for indoor storage of less than 100 kilograms of Class I materials. The indoor storage rooms should have approved self-closing fire doors and protected windows as described in OSHA regulations.

For indoor storage of quantities of between 100 and 1,000 kilograms of Class I flammable liquids, it is anticipated that from one to five storage cabinets would be needed. For indoor storage of the same quantities of hazardous materials, there could be one or multiple lockers. The only restriction is that lockers cannot exceed 1,500 square feet of gross floor area. A maximum of three storage cabinets are permitted in one fire area (likely a

---

[42] Note that this assumption is made solely for the purposes of the environmental consequences analysis. The DOJ COPS Office is not precluding any specific storage unit configuration. Specific limitations applicable to storage units depend upon the types and amounts of hazardous waste stored in the units and the length of time that the hazardous wastes are stored in the units.

separate room) which is defined as a building area separated from the rest of the building by construction having a fire resistance of at least one hour. For example, for indoor storage of 500 kilograms of flammables and 500 kilograms of hazardous materials (a total of 1,000 kilograms), the storage scenario would be one fire area containing 3 storage cabinets (total 600 kilogram capacity for the 3 cabinets) and another fire area containing sufficient hazardous materials lockers (depending on size of each locker) to accommodate 500 kilograms capacity. The DOJ COPS Office assumes that the fire areas would be 400 square feet in area to accommodate the storage units. With this size fire area, the walls, ceiling, and floors would need to have a 2-hour fire resistance instead of the usual 1-hour fire resistance for smaller rooms. In this case, for indoor storage of less than 1,000 kilograms, no additional special fire protection such as sprinklers or water sprays would be needed other than those needed for the building in general.

The indoor storage area could also have quantities greater than 1,000 kilograms, for a grantee operating as a large quantity generator. For this scenario, the DOJ COPS Office assumes that 1,500 kilograms of storage capacity would be needed. For indoor storage of 1,500 kilograms of Class I flammable liquids, it is anticipated that seven storage cabinets would be sufficient. For the same quantity of hazardous materials, there could be one or multiple lockers. The only restriction is that lockers cannot exceed 1,500 square feet of gross floor area. A maximum of three storage cabinets are permitted in one fire area. If both flammable and hazardous materials were present, the cabinets and lockers would need to be located in separate fire areas. For example, for 750 kilograms of flammables and 750 kilograms of hazardous materials (total of 1,500 kilograms), the storage scenario would be two fire areas containing 3 and 2 storage cabinets respectively, (total 1,000 kilogram capacity for the 5 cabinets) and another fire area containing sufficient hazardous materials lockers (depending on size of locker) to accommodate the 750 kilograms capacity and potential incompatibilities of some of the hazardous materials. The DOJ COPS Office assumes in this case that the fire areas would be 400 square feet in area to accommodate the storage units. With this size fire area, the walls, ceiling, and floors would need to have 2-hour fire resistance instead of the usual 1-hour fire resistance for smaller rooms. In this case, for more than 1,000 kilograms, no additional special fire protection such as sprinklers or water sprays would be needed other than those needed for the building in general.

6.5.2 Outdoor Storage Unit Scenario

Storage units may also be situated at outdoor locations on existing government-owned facility property (e.g., fire stations, police stations.) The DOJ COPS Office has assumed that the outdoor storage units would be prefabricated hazardous materials storage cabinets purchased and shipped to the facility and situated on paved areas (e.g., parking areas, loading docks). The DOJ COPS Office anticipates that the storage units would be dedicated to storage of hazardous waste, and that other hazardous materials used at the facility (e.g., paint, solvents) would not be stored in the same enclosure or adjacent to the enclosed area.[43] The DOJ COPS Office assumes that outdoor storage units would be

---

[43] Note that this assumption is made solely for the purposes of the environmental consequences analysis.

segregated and secured from other outdoor areas of the facility by permanent fixtures (e.g., fences, gates) with required signage indicating the presence of hazardous materials, and that only authorized and qualified personnel would have access to the storage units. Outdoor units would be equipped with fire protection and spill containment systems in accordance with grant award conditions and fire protection and building codes. Fire protection codes applicable to outdoor storage of flammable and hazardous materials (including hazardous wastes) are summarized in Section 5.3.

For outdoor storage of less than 100 kilograms of flammable and hazardous materials, there would likely be two hazardous materials lockers to address potential material incompatibilities. For a small area where the hazardous wastes are stored (less than and equal to 100 square feet) to accommodate small amounts of hazardous wastes, distances between lockers would be a minimum of 5 feet, the distance to the property line would be a minimum of 10 feet and the distance to a public street would be a minimum of 5 feet.

For outdoor storage of between 100 and 1000 kilograms, there would likely be three hazardous materials lockers (depending on the locker size) to accommodate the greater quantities and the potential material incompatibilities. For quantities much greater than 1,000 kilograms, there might be 3-5 hazardous materials lockers (depending on the size of the locker). For a large area where the hazardous materials are stored (>500 feet and <1,500 feet) to accommodate large amounts of hazardous materials, the distances between lockers would be a minimum of 5 feet, distance to the property line would be a minimum of 30 feet and the distance to a public street would be a minimum of 20 feet. For all scenarios, fire control devices such as small hose or portable fire extinguishers would need to be available in the vicinity of the storage area.

6.6   Solid Waste Generation

The DOJ COPS Office anticipates that most grant-funded removal actions would be classified under the CESQG definition. Hazardous waste generated by CESQGs is not required under RCRA to be disposed of in Subtitle C permitted RCRA hazardous waste disposal facilities, but may be disposed at non-RCRA permitted facilities, including municipal or industrial solid waste management facilities and other state-permitted facilities. However, many state hazardous waste regulations require that hazardous wastes generated by CESQGs be disposed of in RCRA Subtitle C-permitted TSDFs and thereby prohibit disposal of such wastes in municipal or industrial solid waste management facilities.[44] DOJ COPS Office Certification of Cleanup of Clandestine Drug Laboratories (FY2002) Form specifies that under the Methamphetamine Initiative qualified law enforcement personnel and qualified hazardous waste management contractor personnel utilize permitted treatment, storage, and disposal facilities that meet RCRA requirements to manage hazardous wastes generated from grant-funded activities. This would not

---

The DOJ COPS Office is not precluding any specific storage unit configuration. Specific limitations applicable to storage units depend upon the types and amounts of hazardous waste stored in the units and the length of time that the hazardous wastes are store in the units.

[44] States that require disposal of CESQG-generated waste in RCRA-permitted TSDFs include California, Colorado, Georgia, Kentucky, Illinois, Louisiana, Minnesota, Nebraska, New Mexico, and Wisconsin.

prohibit disposal of CESQG-generated wastes in non-RCRA Subtitle C permitted facilities, in states where such disposal is permitted. DEA prohibits its hazardous waste management contractors from disposing of CESQG-generated waste in non-RCRA permitted facilities. Hazardous wastes generated by agencies classified as SQGs or LQGs are required under RCRA to dispose of such wastes in RCRA Subtitle C-permitted TSDFs.

DEA contractors are required to manage all hazardous materials removed from clandestine drug laboratories as RCRA-regulated hazardous wastes. The DOJ COPS Office does not require grantees conducting grant-funded removal actions to manage all wastes removed from the sites as hazardous waste, and such wastes may be segregated from and managed separately from non-hazardous wastes recovered from the laboratory sites. This DEA requirement reduces the potential for DEA contractors to inadvertently misclassify hazardous waste recovered from clandestine drug laboratories as non-hazardous waste. Misclassification of hazardous waste as non-hazardous waste could result in disposal of such waste at disposal facilities that are not permitted to accept hazardous waste.

Some grantees have used grant funding to pay commercial disposal fees to permitted hazardous waste treatment, storage, and disposal facilities state-permitted treatment and disposal facilities for disposal of hazardous wastes generated from grant-funded removal actions. Operation of permitted treatment and disposal facilities is not addressed in the quantitative environmental consequences analyses in this Environmental Assessment. The DOJ COPS Office assumes that environmental consequences of operation of treatment and disposal facilities utilized to dispose of grantee-generated hazardous wastes have already been assessed through the siting and permitting process for such facilities, including environmental reviews required under NEPA and state regulations. The DOJ COPS Office anticipates that the addition of hazardous waste from removal actions to treatment and disposal facilities would not significantly affect the environmental consequences of such facilities.

6.7   *Other Grant-funded Activities*

This section describes other grant-funded activities not directly related to hazardous waste removal actions that could have potential environmental impacts. These activities include but are not limited to grant-funded training activities, seizures of clandestine laboratories, chemical analytical laboratory operations, including analysis of evidence and environmental samples, on-site environmental monitoring activities, and clandestine drug laboratory on-site investigation and law enforcement activities.

Training activities generates hazardous waste in the form of chemical laboratory apparatus and chemicals used by trainers and students to conduct practical exercises. Generation of hazardous wastes from training activities includes glassware, flammable substances (e.g., automotive starter fluid (ether), methanol), corrosives, (e.g., sulfuric acid), and reactives (e.g., lithium batteries).[45] The DOJ COPS Office anticipates that agencies and contractors

---

[45] Arkansas State Police ORI# ARASP1300, Section B Project Summary, "Supplies for Practical Exercise

conducting grant-funded training would not generate more than 100 kilograms of waste in a calendar month, and would therefore operate as CESQGs. However, it is possible that some training providers could operate as SQGs.

Conduct of clandestine drug laboratory seizure operations and removal actions also may generate other types of hazardous waste in addition to the hazardous chemicals recovered from the clandestine drug laboratory itself. Clandestine drug laboratory investigation and law enforcement operations and removal actions may result in generation of other types of hazardous wastes, including contaminated personal protective equipment, equipment (consumables) used to conduct site environmental and occupational health and safety monitoring, site surveillance, and collection of evidence, and potentially also liquids used on site to decontaminate hazardous waste-contaminated personnel and equipment. The DOJ COPS Office anticipates that agencies conducting grant-funded clandestine drug laboratory seizures would not generate more than 100 kilograms of such hazardous wastes in a calendar month, however, agencies involved in seizures of a large number of clandestine drug laboratories or that encounter "superlabs" for which seizures involve extensive use of personal protective equipment and consumables could generate more than 100 kilograms of hazardous waste in a calendar month.

Grantees also have used grant funding to outfit, equip, and staff chemical analytical laboratories that are used to analyze evidence and environmental samples taken at clandestine drug laboratory sites. Analysis of evidence and environmental samples obtained during clandestine drug laboratory seizures may also be conducted on site, depending upon the specific types of samples and analyses being conducted. In either case, hazardous wastes generated from analysis of evidence and environmental samples may include contaminated glassware, spent chemical reagents, used personal protective equipment, and other consumables.

7.0   Affected Environment

This section describes the environmental setting for scenarios for which environmental consequence analyses were conducted. The environmental setting includes a general description of the air quality, water quality, soil quality, floodplains and wetlands, human health and safety, and social setting for each scenario. This section also briefly describes elements of the environment that are unlikely to be affected by the Proposed Action and the rationale for excluding such elements from the environmental consequence analyses.

7.1   *Single Family House Environmental Setting*

The single-family house for the Single Family House Removal Action Scenario is assumed to be located in a residential neighborhood, 50 feet from the closest adjacent residence. Hazardous waste containers are assumed to be situated both inside the house and in the backyard. The house and backyard are assumed not to be located in the immediate vicinity of a wetland or stream or other water body, or in the vicinity of any

"Meth Cook."

threatened or endangered species habitat. The air quality inside the single-family house is assumed to be degraded by the operation of the clandestine drug laboratory and presence of hazardous air indoor air pollutants, but baseline concentrations of hazardous indoor air pollutants are assumed not to represent an acute hazard or immediate danger to life or health. Surface soils in the area surrounding the house and backyard area are assumed to be contaminated by previously released hazardous waste; however, baseline concentrations in soil are assumed not to represent an acute hazard or immediate danger to life or health.

7.2   Multi-Unit Residential Property Environmental Setting

For the Multi-unit Residential Property Scenario, the dwelling unit in which the clandestine drug laboratory is situated is assumed to be located in multi-story multi-unit residential building, adjacent to other occupied units. The air quality inside the dwelling unit is assumed to be degraded by operation of the clandestine drug laboratory and the presence of hazardous air indoor air pollutants, but baseline concentrations of hazardous indoor air pollutants are assumed not to represent an acute hazard or immediate danger to life or health. It is further assumed that the air quality of adjacent dwelling units has not been affected by operation of the clandestine drug laboratory, (*i.e.,* no releases of hazardous wastes from previous operation of the clandestine drug laboratory have affected the air quality of any adjacent dwelling units). There is assumed to be no significant potential for surface soil or surface water contamination associated with this scenario, because the clandestine drug laboratory and associated hazardous materials are situated within a dwelling unit of a multi-story building. Any liquid releases of hazardous wastes from the dwelling unit are assumed to be entrained to municipal storm water management systems connected to a Publicly Owned Treatment Works (POTW).

7.3   Rural Open Air Setting Environmental Setting

The clandestine drug laboratory for the Rural Open Air Setting Scenario is assumed to contain no buildings or other permanent structures, such that any containers and apparatus are unsecured and any releases of hazardous wastes from the site would be uncontained. The site is assumed to be in the vicinity of surface water, wetlands, and vegetation and potentially in the vicinity of habitat of threatened or endangered species. It is assumed that the topography of the site is such that any hazardous waste releases or storm water runoff (and any entrained hazardous wastes) would flow towards a nearby surface water body, including wetlands areas, and that baseline water quality in the surface water body and wetlands areas have been affected by previous operation of the clandestine drug laboratory, (*i.e.,* there have been previous releases of hazardous wastes that have affected surface water quality). Surface soils in the area of the site are assumed to be contaminated by previously released hazardous wastes; however, baseline soil concentrations are assumed not to represent an acute hazard or immediate danger to life or health.

In the DOJ COPS Office's experience, contamination of groundwater as a result of hazardous waste releases at a clandestine drug laboratory location, while possible, is very unlikely to occur, and therefore the potential for groundwater contamination not assessed quantitatively. Hazardous wastes releases from clandestine drug laboratory locations under the Rural Open Air Setting are more likely to result in soil or surface water contamination.

7.4   *Storage Scenarios*

7.4.1   Indoor Storage Scenario

It is assumed that the transfer stations used by DEA contractors are located in enclosed buildings that are situated in industrial-zoned areas in accordance with local zoning laws, and that there are residential structures 200 feet of the transfer stations. It is also assumed that baseline indoor air quality meets occupational health and safety standards and that baseline outdoor air quality meets federal and state air quality standards. It is also assumed that the transfer station is equipped with containment structures would contain any releases of liquid hazardous wastes from the transfer station, and that any air releases resulting from releases of gaseous or volatile hazardous wastes would be ventilated to the atmosphere through gravity or mechanical ventilation systems. It is assumed that hazardous waste contractor personnel are the only individuals permitted to handle hazardous waste in the storage unit, and that only hazardous waste contractor personnel work in the vicinity of the storage unit.

It is assumed that other storage units utilized by grantees would be located in existing government-owned buildings situated in mixed-use-zoned areas in accordance with local zoning laws, and that there are residential structures 50 feet from the building. It is assumed that baseline indoor air quality meets occupational health and safety standards and that outdoor air quality meets federal and state air quality standards. It is also assumed that any liquid hazardous waste releases from the storage unit would be partially contained by the building structure and any associated containment systems. In accordance with NFPA Code 30, storage units may or may not have dedicated ventilation systems to the outside of the building, but would not be vented to inside the building. It is assumed that qualified and authorized personnel are the only individuals permitted to handle hazardous waste in the storage unit, but that non-trained personnel also work in the vicinity of the storage unit.

7.4.2   Outdoor Storage Scenario

It is assumed that storage units utilized by grantees would be located outside an existing government-owned building that is situated in mixed-use-zoned areas in accordance with local zoning laws, and that there are residential structures 50 feet from the building. It is assumed that baseline outdoor air quality meets federal and state air quality standards. It is also assumed that paved areas upon which the storage unit is situated would at least partially contain liquid releases and that any air releases resulting from hazardous waste releases or fire could directly affect adjacent properties subject to wind direction. It is assumed that qualified and authorized personnel are the only individuals permitted to handle hazardous waste in the storage unit, but that non-trained personnel also work in the vicinity of the storage unit.

8.0 Environmental Consequences

This section describes environmental consequences analyses for the DOJ COPS Office Methamphetamine Initiative (the Proposed Action) and No Action Alternative.

8.1 DOJ COPS Office Methamphetamine Initiative

This section describes the environmental consequences analysis for the DOJ COPS Office Methamphetamine Initiative for the Proposed Action, including "grant-funded hazardous waste management activities" and "other grant-funded activities." Included in hazardous waste management activities are the two removal action scenarios, one transportation scenario, and three storage scenarios.

8.1.1 Air Quality

Hazardous Waste Management Activities

Air quality benefits are anticipated from the normal conduct of removal actions under the DOJ COPS Office Methamphetamine Initiative. Clandestine drug laboratories represent a continuing source of air emissions from hazardous wastes stored at the sites, including containers and apparatus and furnishings that may be contaminated with hazardous wastes or controlled substance residues. Conduct of grant-funded removal actions, including the packaging and removal of the hazardous wastes from the laboratory site, would result in the reduction in existing air emissions from the clandestine drug laboratory operation. The DOJ COPS Office assumes that all removal actions will be conducted in accordance with state and federal requirements (summarized in Section 5) and DOJ COPS Office grant award conditions (summarized in Appendices C, D, and E).

The DOJ COPS Office anticipates that concentrations of air contaminants may exist within and in the vicinity of clandestine drug laboratories during seizure operations and during removal actions that may require the use of personal protective equipment by personnel conducting the seizure operations and removal actions. Potential impacts related to potential occupational exposure during normal conduct of seizure operations and removal actions are discussed below in Section 8.1.4 (Health and Safety.). Potential impacts related to potential accidental releases of hazardous wastes during conduct of removal actions are discussed in this section.

Removal Action Scenarios

The air quality impact analysis for potential accidental releases during conduct of a removal action is based on an assumed accidental release involving 100 kilograms of anhydrous ammonia gas. Such a release could occur as a result of a materials handling accident or container failure during a removal action. The DOJ COPS Office considers the probability of such an occurrence to be low, however, such a release could occur during the conduct of a removal action. EPA has reported that brass valving of illicit containers containing anhydrous ammonia that appeared to be physically intact from outside appearance has been known to break off in the hands of responders creating an uncontrolled release from the container.[46] The potential consequences of such a release could be significant. The detailed methodology and assumptions for determining air quality impacts associated with accidental releases for the DOJ COPS Office Methamphetamine Initiative removal action scenarios are provided in Appendix K, Methodology for Assessing Potential Consequences of Hazardous Waste Air Releases.

The specific consequences of an accidental release vary for an indoor release or outdoor release for the Single-Family House Scenario and for an indoor release for the Multi-unit Dwelling Scenario with respect to the potential for public or occupational exposure. The potential consequences for an outdoor release for the Rural Open Air Scenario would not exceed the potential consequences for an outdoor release for the Single Family House Scenario; therefore no separate quantitative analysis has been conducted for an outdoor release for the Rural Open Air Scenario.

Single Family House Scenario

If 100 kilograms of anhydrous ammonia gas were released inside the single-family house (30,000 cubic feet), the anticipated ammonia concentration initially would be 160,000 ppm. This concentration could be fatal to persons conducting the removal action in the house and exposed to the ammonia release, unless they were wearing personal protective equipment or removed from the situation by emergency responders. The OSHA Immediately Dangerous to Life or Health (IDLH) level for anhydrous ammonia is 300 ppm for workers for a 30-minute exposure.

Assuming that 55% of the released ammonia escapes from the building (see Appendix K for an explanation of this assumption) the indoor ammonia concentration inside the nearest residence, assumed to be 50 feet away, would equal the ERPG-2 level of 150 ppm. As a result, persons in this nearby house would experience health effects, but not irreversible or other serious health effects or symptoms that would impair their ability to take protective action. The dispersion modeling also indicated that persons that located outside and at a location 100 feet from the point of release would experience the same ERPG-2 level concentration and experience its corresponding health effects.
If 100 kilograms of anhydrous ammonia gas were released outside the single family house, the ammonia would disperse so that residents inside houses 50 feet away from the point of release would experience ammonia concentrations greater than the ERPG-2 level of 150 ppm, and residents inside houses 75 feet away from the point of release would experience ammonia concentrations equal to the ERPG-2 level. As a result, persons in nearby residences would experience health effects, but not irreversible or other serious health effects or symptoms that would impair their ability to take protective action. The dispersion modeling also indicated that persons located outside and at 130 feet from the point of release would experience the same ERPG –2 level concentration and experience its corresponding health effects.[47] For the rural open-air scenario, human receptors

---

[46] EPA, 2000. Anhydrous Ammonia Theft, United States Environmental Protection Agency, Office of Solid Waste and Emergency Response, (5104), EPA Publication Number EPA-F-00-005, March 2000, http://www.epa.gov/ceppo/pubs/csalert.pdf
[47] For the Rural Open Air scenario, human receptors located 130 feet from the point of outdoor release

located 130 feet from the point of an outdoor release would experience the same ERPG-2 level concentration as for the outdoor release for the single-family house scenario.

Multi-unit Residential Property Scenario

If 100 kilograms of anhydrous ammonia gas were released inside an apartment (15,000 cubic feet) in a multi-unit residential property, the anticipated ammonia concentration initially would be 320,000 parts per million (ppm). This concentration could be fatal to persons conducting the removal action in the dwelling and exposed to the ammonia release, unless they were wearing personal protective equipment or removed from the situation by emergency responders. Assuming that 55% of the ammonia escapes from the apartment into adjacent apartments, the adjacent apartments could be expected to have ammonia concentrations of approximately 6,400 ppm. This concentration far exceeds the ERPG-2 level of 150 ppm, and exposure to such concentration would impair the ability of persons to take protective action. As a result, persons in adjacent apartments would experience severe health effects. Table 8.1-1 summarizes air quality impacts for the removal action scenarios.

Table 8.1-1
Potential Air Quality Impacts for Ammonia Release for Removal Action Scenarios

Scenario	Event	Ammonia Concentration^	Exposure Guideline		Distance to Concentration
Single Family House	Indoor Release	160,000 ppm	300 ppm	IDLH Occupational Exposure Guideline	Point of Release
Single Family House	Indoor Release Adjacent House	150 ppm	150 ppm	ERPG-2 Public Exposure Guideline	50 Feet*
Single Family House	Indoor Release Outdoor Receptor	150 ppm	150 ppm	ERPG-2 Public Exposure Guideline	100 Feet
Single Family House	Outdoor Release Adjacent House	370 ppm	150 ppm	ERPG-2 Public Exposure Guideline	50 Feet
Single Family House	Outdoor Release Adjacent House	150 ppm	150 ppm	ERPG-2 Public Exposure Guideline	75 Feet
Single Family House	Outdoor Release Outdoor Receptor	150 ppm	150 ppm	ERPG-2 Public Exposure Guideline	130 Feet
Multi-Unit Dwelling	Indoor Release	320,000 ppm	300 ppm	IDLH Occupational Exposure Guideline	Point of Release
Multi-Unit Dwelling	Indoor Release	6,400 ppm	150 ppm	ERPG-2 Public Exposure Guideline	Adjacent Apartment
Rural Open Air	Outdoor Release Outdoor Receptor	150 ppm	150 ppm	ERPG-2 Public Exposure Guideline	130 Feet

Notes: ^Exposure times for ERPG and IDLH are 60 minutes and 30 minutes, respectively.
Concentrations are calculated for the respective exposure time.
*The closest occupied structure is assumed to be located 50 feet from the single-family house.

Transportation Scenario

Air quality impacts from the normal transportation of the recovered hazardous waste to the storage units under the DOJ COPS Office Methamphetamine Initiative are anticipated

would experience the same ERPG-2 level concentration as for the outdoor release in the Single Family House scenario.

to be negligible, assuming that the hazardous wastes are packaged, handled, transported, and stored by qualified personnel in accordance with Federal and state regulations and grant award conditions. Air quality impacts from the operation of vehicles used to transport the hazardous waste are negligible with respect to overall transportation traffic.

The air quality impacts of an uncontrolled release during a transportation accident of 100 kilograms of anhydrous ammonia are similar to those associated with the removal action scenarios. It is assumed that an accident occurs involving a transportation vehicle conveying hazardous waste from the removal action, which results in a container breach. The detailed methodology and assumptions for determining air quality impacts associated with an accidental release during a transportation accident are presented in Appendix K and summarized in Table 8.1-2.

Similar to the removal action scenario, the primary exposed individuals would be the qualified law enforcement personnel or contractors operating the vehicle as well as any passengers in the vehicle. The secondary exposed individuals would be any public individuals in the vicinity of the release. The DOJ COPS Office has assumed for the transportation scenario, the nearest exposed public individual is 50 feet from the point of release (e.g. a residence near the accident location), the same distance assumed for the removal action scenarios. Thus, the DOJ COPS Office assumes that the dispersion modeling results for air quality impacts would be the same for the removal action outdoor release scenario as for the transportation accident scenario.

Table 8.1-2
Potential Air Quality Impacts for Ammonia Release for Transportation Scenario

Scenario	Event	Ammonia Concentration^	Exposure Guideline		Distance to Concentration
Transportation	Transportation Release Indoor Receptor	150 ppm	150 ppm	ERPG-2 Public Exposure Guideline	75 Feet
Transportation	Transportation Release Outdoor Receptor	150 ppm	150 ppm	ERPG-2 Public Exposure Guideline	130 Feet

Notes: ^Exposure times for ERPG and IDLH are 60 minutes and 30 minutes, respectively. Concentrations are calculated for the respective exposure time.
*The closest public individual is assumed to be located 50 feet from the transportation incident

The likelihood of a release and timeliness and effectiveness of emergency response may be affected by the mode of transportation and specific regulatory requirements. CESQG's transporting CESQG-generated wastes are not required under RCRA to utilize vehicle placards, hazardous waste container markings, or hazardous waste manifests. DEA contractors are required comply with RCRA regulations for SQGs, including utilization of manifests, container markings, and vehicle placards, regardless of the quantity transported. Other transporters transporting CESQG waste may or may not placard, mark, or manifest shipments, but may instead use shipping papers that may not provide the same information to responders. In the event that a vehicle transporting hazardous waste without placards, container markings, or manifests is involved in an accident, responders to the accident would not necessarily be aware of the chemical hazards to which the driver, passengers or members of the public had been exposed. The driver and any passengers could be exposed to a "point of release" concentration (i.e. orders of magnitude higher than the IDLH), which could impair the ability of the driver and passengers to take protective action.

EPA reported that emergency responders and members of the public were exposed to anhydrous ammonia as a consequence of a transportation accident. In May 1999, a vehicle passenger was killed when a makeshift 20-pound container of anhydrous ammonia he was holding exploded inside a vehicle. The death occurred when two individuals were driving on an interstate highway in Missouri. The driver of the vehicle was severely injured. The anhydrous ammonia being transported was to be used for methamphetamine production. The cause of the smoke emanating from the vehicle was not immediately known, and therefore one firefighter, one emergency medical technician, and one member of the general public, all of whom stopped to help and drag the driver and passenger from the car, were also injured as a result of the ammonia release.[48]

Storage Scenarios

Under the Proposed Action, hazardous waste generated from removal actions may be stored either indoors or outdoors in storage units, including grantee- or contractor-operated transfer stations or permitted storage facilities. A storage unit where hazardous waste for less than ten days, in transit to a treatment and disposal facility, is classified as a "transfer station" and is subject to a limited number of RCRA requirements. Transfer stations do not require RCRA permits. Table 5.1-1 summarizes the regulatory requirements for less than ten-day transfer stations.

A storage unit where hazardous waste is stored for more than ten days would be classified as a "storage facility" that would require a RCRA hazardous waste storage permit and would be required to comply with RCRA regulations for hazardous waste storage facilities. A permitted RCRA hazardous waste storage facility would be required to have full secondary containment systems for spills and would be required to implement an inspection plan, which would not be required for less than 10-day storage. Table 5.1-1 summarizes the regulatory requirements for a RCRA permitted storage facility. As discussed in Section 5.1, the regulatory requirements for management of quantities between 100 and 1000 kilograms and greater than 1000 kilograms differ from the regulatory requirements applicable to CESQGs, and requirements differ for storage of hazardous waste for less than or more than 10 days,

Indoor Storage Scenario

In the event that 100 kilograms of anhydrous ammonia were released inside a storage unit that was located inside an assumed 60,000 cubic foot building (e.g., an indoor storage unit

---

[48] EPA, 2000. Anhydrous Ammonia Theft, United States Environmental Protection Agency, Office of Solid Waste and Emergency Response, (5104), EPA Publication Number EPA-F-00-005, March 2000. http://www.epa.gov/ceppo/pubs/csalert.pdf

at a fire station or police station or contractor-operated transfer station), the ammonia gas would escape from the building through the ventilation system of the storage unit, if the unit were equipped with a ventilation system. If the storage unit were not equipped with a ventilation system, the ammonia release would escape into the building. An ammonia release that resulted from a materials handling accident inside the building but outside the storage unit would also escape into the building. In either case the anticipated ammonia concentration inside a 60,000 cubic foot building initially would be 80,000 parts per million, exceeding the IDLH level of 300 ppm for a 30-minute exposure. Personnel would not be able to function in this environment unless they had personal protective equipment.

Assuming that 55% of the ammonia released into the building escapes from the building and into the ambient air, dispersion modeling of the ammonia indicates that a residence or commercial entity located 50 feet from the point of the release would experience indoor ammonia concentrations equal to the ERPG-2 level of 150 ppm for ammonia. As a result, persons in this nearby building would experience health effects, but not irreversible or other serious health effects or symptoms that would impair their ability to take protective action. The dispersion modeling also indicated that persons located outside and at 100 feet from the point of release would experience the same ERPG-2 level concentration and experience its corresponding health effects.

Outdoor Storage Scenario

In the event that the storage unit was located outside of building (e.g., outside of a police station or fire station,) all of the ammonia released would escape through the ventilation system of the unit. The ammonia would disperse so that occupants of buildings up to 75 feet from the point of release would experience indoor ammonia concentrations equal to the ERPG-2 level of 150 ppm for ammonia. As a result, occupants of these buildings would experience health effects, but not irreversible or other serious health effects or symptoms that would impair their ability to take protective action. The dispersion modeling also indicated that persons located outside and at 130 feet from the point of release would experience the same ERPG-2 level concentration and experience its corresponding health effects. Potential air quality impacts associated with the indoor and outdoor storage scenarios are summarized in Table 8.1-3.

Table 8.1-3
Potential Air Quality Impacts for Ammonia Release for Storage Scenarios

Scenario	Event	Ammonia Concentration^	Exposure Guideline		Distance to Concentration
Storage Unit	Normal Operation	Negligible	300 ppm	IDLH Occupational Exposure Guideline	Immediate Vicinity
Storage Unit – Indoor Unit	Accidental Release Indoor Receptor	80,000 ppm	300 ppm	IDLH Occupational Exposure Guideline	Point of Release
	Accidental Release Indoor Receptor	150 ppm	150 ppm	ERPG-2 Public Exposure Guideline	50 Feet*

Storage Unit -- Indoor Unit	Accidental Release Outdoor Receptor	530 ppm	150 ppm	ERPG-2 Public Exposure Guideline	50 Feet *
	Accidental Release Outdoor Receptor	150 ppm	150 ppm	ERPG-2 Public Exposure Guideline	100 Feet
Storage Unit – Indoor Unit Transfer Station	Accidental Release Outdoor Receptor	75 ppm	150 ppm	ERPG-2 Public Exposure Guideline	200 Feet**
Storage Unit – Outdoor Unit	Accidental Release Indoor Receptor	370 ppm	150 ppm	ERPG-2 Public Exposure Guideline	50 Feet*
	Accidental Release Indoor Receptor	150 ppm	150 ppm	ERPG-2 Public Exposure Guideline	75 Feet
Storage Unit – Outdoor Unit	Accidental Release Outdoor Receptor	970 ppm	150 ppm	ERPG-2 Public Exposure Guideline	50 Feet*
	Accidental Release Outdoor Receptor	150 ppm	150 ppm	ERPG-2 Public Exposure Guideline	130 Feet

Notes: ^Exposure times for ERPG and IDLH are 60 minutes and 30 minutes, respectively. Concentrations are calculated for the respective exposure time. These air quality impacts are estimated based on a ground level release and do not account for the characteristics of building ventilation systems. Storage units may be equipped with ventilation systems, and buildings may be equipped with gravity or mechanical ventilation systems that would reduce to some extent indoor and outdoor air concentrations.

*The closest occupied structure is assumed to be located 50 feet from the storage unit location.
**The closest occupied structure is assumed to be located 200 feet from the transfer station.

Storage of greater than 100 kilogram quantities

Grantees may encounter quantities of hazardous waste greater than 100 kilograms, or greater than 1,000 kilograms, in conducting clandestine drug laboratory seizures and removal actions. Such hazardous wastes would be classified as SQG or LQG wastes, and transportation of such wastes to storage units would require a RCRA transporter license. Storage of these quantities by a grantee meeting state and federal regulatory requirements and DOJ COPS Office Award Conditions would be allowed under the Proposed Action. However, the DOJ COPS Office has assumed it to be unlikely that in the event that a grantee stored greater than 100 kilograms of hazardous waste in a single location that an accidental release would involve the entire quantity of stored hazardous waste at that location. The DOJ COPS Office anticipates that a release of the entire quantity of stored hazardous waste from a single location as a result of breaching of all stored containers at once would only occur in the event of a facility-wide fire. This situation is possible but highly unlikely, considering that storage of hazardous wastes generated by SQGs or LQGs would be subject to additional regulatory requirements that do not apply to CESQG-generated hazardous waste. The DOJ COPS Office therefore has not performed any quantitative analysis of potential environmental consequences of potential releases of greater than 100 kilograms of hazardous waste.

In general, an outdoor release of greater than 100 kilograms of hazardous waste would result in higher concentrations persisting over greater distances and for longer periods than for a 100-kilogram release. Therefore, the radius of potential exceedance of ERPG-2 levels would increase for a larger quantity release, potentially increasing the number of exposed public receptors depending upon the location of the accidental release. With respect to indoor releases, the point of release concentration to which persons within the building would be exposed would increase in a linear manner with the quantity of release, without accounting for any differences in the characteristics of storage unit or building ventilation systems.

Other Grant Funded Activities

Grant-funded training could potentially result in an impact to air quality. Several states use DOJ COPS Office funding for laboratory demonstrations of how methamphetamine is chemically produced and the specific precursor chemicals involved. The State of Arkansas Initiative, for example, provides a grant-funded training program to familiarize its agents with the methamphetamine cooking process and precursors. Use of chemicals in training activities would result in fugitive air emissions. However, the quantities of chemicals utilized for training are low and are used by trainers in a controlled environment. Air emissions associated with grant-funded training are therefore not anticipated to significantly affect ambient air quality or to result in occupational exposure of trainees.

Grant funding has been used to purchase vehicles for the transportation of personnel, safety and law enforcement equipment and hazardous waste. Vehicles purchased using grant funding have included automobiles, full sized pickup trucks, clandestine laboratory "response vehicles" that are designed to carry safety equipment and that may be equipped with personnel decontamination apparatus, and all-terrain vehicles. Operation of vehicles has potential environmental impacts with respect to vehicle air emissions.

In general, grant-funded vehicles are used to consolidate transportation of personnel and safety equipment to clandestine drug laboratory locations and may therefore result in operation of fewer vehicles and reduction in vehicle miles traveled, or reduction in emissions per vehicle mile. Vehicles are also used to transport hazardous waste from clandestine drug laboratory locations. However, some of the vehicles being purchased are full sized pickup trucks, SUVs with towing packages, and off-road vehicles including all-terrain vehicles. Some of the vehicles are replacing smaller vehicles or are replacing older vehicles. However, the availability of additional vehicles may result in increased law enforcement activities, potentially increasing vehicle miles traveled. Overall however, operation of grant-funded vehicles would not represent a significant source of air emissions as compared to overall agency vehicle operations.

The DOJ COPS Office Methamphetamine Initiative also may result in increased air emissions from operation of chemical analytical laboratories. These analytical laboratories process evidence and environmental samples from seized clandestine drug laboratories. Grants are used to purchase additional analytic equipment such as scanning electron microscopes and general laboratory supplies such as glassware and chemical analytical reagents. Grants may also fund the training of additional analytical chemists. Typical air emissions from an analytical laboratory are not anticipated to significantly affect air quality. For most grant-funded methamphetamine initiatives, the chemical analytical laboratories are already constructed and operating independently of the initiative, and grant funding is used to supplement existing operations. Therefore any grant-funded equipment or personnel would only result in an incremental increase over existing air emissions from the laboratory facility. The DOJ COPS Office grants would generally only provide equipment, supplies, and personnel, not construction or modification of buildings or structures, and the DOJ COPS Office does not anticipate providing grant funding to establish an entirely new chemical analytical laboratory under the Proposed Action. Any new construction or modification of a chemical analytical laboratory would be subject to site-specific NEPA analysis and is outside the scope of the Proposed Action.

8.1.2 Water Quality

Hazardous Waste Management Activities

Removal Action Scenarios

Potential benefits to water quality are anticipated from the normal conduct of removal actions under the DOJ COPS Office Methamphetamine Initiative. Clandestine drug laboratories represent a potential source of releases to surface water from hazardous wastes stored and used at the sites. Conduct of grant-funded removal actions would reduce potential sources of releases to surface water from clandestine drug laboratory operations, including illicit releases of hazardous wastes to sinks, drains, or outdoor areas. Such releases could contaminate surface water directly or affect the operation of septic systems or POTW.

Normal conduct of laboratory seizures and removal actions could involve generation of wastewater from the operation of grant-funded portable decontamination stations used to decontaminate personnel conducting operations. It is assumed that decontamination wastewater is not released to the environment at the removal action location but is collected and disposed of in accordance with federal, state, and local requirements and DOJ COPS Office grant award conditions. No significant environmental impacts to water quality are anticipated for normal conduct of removal actions.

Single Family House Scenario / Rural Open Air Setting Scenario

An accidental release during a removal action conducting in an outdoor environment for the Single Family House or Rural Open Air Setting scenarios could result in potential environmental impacts to surface water. A release of hazardous waste to surface water, either directly or indirectly through runoff, could result from a materials handling accident or container failure. The DOJ COPS Office considers the probability of such an occurrence to be low, however, the potential consequences of such a release could be significant if the release is not controlled. The potential release of hazardous waste directly to surface water during a removal action is unlikely considering that the personnel conducting the removal action would be available to respond to the release, and the laboratory location may or may not be in the vicinity of a surface water body. Also, a release of hazardous waste to surface soil would likely be diluted on its way to any nearby surface water body and would result in a lower environmental impact than a release directly to surface water.

The DOJ COPS Office conducted dispersion modeling for an uncontrolled release to surface water based on a methodology and data developed by the USGS.[49] The DOJ COPS Office based the release modeling on a potential release of 100 kilograms of either toluene or iodine, based on the amounts of these hazardous wastes found at clandestine drug laboratory sites and the aquatic toxicity of these compounds. Iodine and toluene were selected for the screening water quality analysis based on several factors including that toluene and iodine have been recovered from clandestine drug laboratories in quantities on the order of 100 kilograms for a single site. Surface water quality and aquatic toxicity criteria could be exceeded in rivers and streams in the event of an uncontrolled 100-kilogram release. The consequences of such a release are based on the quantities and characteristics of the hazardous wastes released and the characteristics of the river or stream in which the release occurs. The methodology and results of the surface water release dispersion modeling are shown in Appendix L, Water Quality Impact Analysis.

The Rural Open Air Setting location is assumed to be in the vicinity of a surface water body. A release of a liquid or solid hazardous waste during a laboratory seizure or removal action would be subject to emergency response by removal action personnel trained in emergency response. It is assumed that the response would be timely, but not necessarily totally effective, depending upon the specific response equipment that the hazardous waste management personnel have available. Effectiveness of the response would depend upon the circumstances of the release and the environmental setting of the release, and on the specific equipment that the responders have available. A liquid spill may not be fully contained by emergency response and could result in impacts to surface water quality. By comparison, a solid release (e.g., iodine) could be mostly contained and remediated. It is possible that a liquid release at an urban or suburban location could impact a storm sewer or sanitary sewer system. Such a release would likely enter a municipal wastewater treatment system and could result in potential effects on POTW operation downstream of the release. A liquid release at an outdoor location, if not contained in a timely manner, could have direct impacts to a surface water body.

Multi-unit Residential Property Scenario

Removal action locations for the Multi-unit Residential Property Scenario are assumed not to be situated in the vicinity of a surface water body.

Transportation Scenario

The DOJ COPS Office Methamphetamine Initiative may result in potential impacts to surface water quality associated with transportation of hazardous waste from the removal

---

[49] Jobson, H.E., 1996. Predictions of Travel Time and Longitudinal Dispersion in Rivers and Streams, USGS Water Resources Investigation Report 96-4013, 1996.

action location to the storage location. It is assumed for this scenario that an accident occurs involving a transportation vehicle conveying hazardous waste from the removal action. The accident is assumed to result in a hazardous waste container either entering directly into a stream or hazardous waste from a breached container being inadvertently washed into a stream by emergency response personnel responding to the accident.

The methodology and results of the surface water release dispersion modeling are shown in Appendix L, Water Quality Impact Analysis. The modeling for the transportation scenario assumes the same release quantity and river/stream characteristics as for the removal action scenario, and therefore the modeled concentrations are the same as for the removal action scenario, discussed above. Surface water quality and aquatic toxicity criteria could be exceeded in rivers and streams in the event of an uncontrolled 100-kilogram release.

The likelihood of a release and potential consequences of a release may differ for the self-transportation scenario and the licensed transport scenario, and may be affected by potential differences in release response time and response actions taken by qualified law enforcement personnel conducting hazardous waste transportation versus DEA contractors conducting the transportation. For the self-transport scenario, hazardous waste may be transported by qualified law enforcement personnel in vehicles that are not designed to carry hazardous waste containers, but that are modified to carry hazardous waste containers. For the licensed transport scenario, hazardous waste may be transported in response vehicles that are designed to transport hazardous waste and that may be more fully enclosed than modified vehicles used for self-transport of waste. The likelihood of a container breach in the event of an accident may be somewhat lower in the event that a response vehicle is used to transport the hazardous waste, however, such differences are not readily quantifiable.

Transportation of less than 100 kg

In the event of a 100 kilogram release of iodine at high river flow rate, the peak iodine concentration would also be 69,300 ug/l at a distance of 1.9 kilometers from the point of release, as the modeling approach is independent of the characteristics of the substance released and only considers the quantity released and the characteristics of the river.

Several factors influence the potential for and the consequences of a release of less than 100 kilograms of hazardous waste as a result of a transportation accident. The potential for releases associated with transportation accident of hazardous waste, and associated potential for discharges to surface water may be higher for self-transportation by grantees than for DEA contractors conducting the transportation. Qualified law enforcement personnel would not necessarily develop as high a level of familiarity with hazardous waste management practices and procedures as would DEA contractors. This is because qualified law enforcement personnel may not be conducting such activities on a day-to-day basis as part of their job function, but would be conducting such activities only on an as-needed basis. This may affect the timeliness and/or effectiveness of response to an accident. The likelihood of a release also depends upon the type of vehicle used and the method by which the containers are secured within the vehicle.

The potential for water quality impacts resulting from a transportation accident could be affected by the timeliness of and effectiveness of response to the accident, which in turn may be affected by the types of information available to responders concerning the characteristics of the hazardous waste involved in the accident. Grantees are not required to use placarded vehicles, container markings, or hazardous waste manifests to self transport CESQG waste, but may instead use shipping papers that may not provide the same level of information concerning the nature of the release as would hazardous waste manifests, container markings, and vehicle placards. Therefore, in an accident scenario, responders would not necessarily be aware that there was a release of hazardous waste.

The DOJ COPS Office anticipates that a shipping paper would be included in the grantee's vehicle for CESQG shipments but that the shipping paper may not provide as detailed or as timely information to responders. Information concerning the DOT proper shipping name, hazard class, DOT identification number, and special handling instructions for the hazardous waste, information that would be included on a hazardous waste manifest may not be available to emergency responders if there is no hazardous waste manifest. This could potentially result in a less timely and less effective response. Solid or liquid releases from a transportation accident could be inadvertently washed into surface water by emergency response personnel if the responders are not aware that the vehicle is transporting hazardous waste. Impacts to surface water associated with hazardous waste releases during transport could therefore be higher for qualified law enforcement personnel conducting transportation actions than for DEA contractors conducting the transportation. However, differences in such human factors are not readily quantifiable, and therefore no quantitative analysis of potential differences in release response time and potential effectiveness of response actions taken have been conducted.

Transportation of greater than 100 kilograms

In the case of transportation of greater than 100 kilograms or over 1000 kilograms of hazardous waste, the grantee would be operating as a SQG or LQG, and therefore all DOT and RCRA regulations would apply (see Tables 5.1-1 and 5.2-1 for a summary of specific regulations). Thus, grantees performing their own transportation would be required to obtain hazardous waste transportation licenses and utilize vehicles placards, container markings, and hazardous waste manifests in accordance with RCRA regulations for SQGs. The additional information provided by the vehicle placards and manifests may increase the timeliness and effectiveness of response actions in the event of a transportation accident.

The DOJ COPS Office has assumed for the purposes of the quantitative environmental consequences analysis that only one 100 kilogram container would be breached in the event of an accident, even if the vehicle were transporting multiple containers with a total of more than 100 kilograms of hazardous waste. The DOJ COPS Office assumes that the release of more than one 100-kilograms during a transportation accident is possible, but unlikely. However, the potential exists for solid or liquid releases from a transportation accident to directly enter surface water or be inadvertently washed into surface water by emergency response personnel responding to a transportation accident. Surface water concentrations resulting from a release of more than 100 kilograms would increase in a more or less linear fashion proportional to the amount of the release.

Storage Scenarios

Indoor Storage Scenario

Indoor storage units that are not permitted RCRA storage facilities would be equipped with spill containment systems in accordance with NFPA Codes and OSHA requirements such that liquid releases would be contained within the unit. It is not likely that building itself would be equipped with a full secondary containment system unless the storage unit were a RCRA permitted storage facility, however, the DOJ COPS Office anticipates that the storage cabinets and lockers would provide containment of releases within the cabinets and lockers. If the storage unit were a RCRA permitted storage facility, it would be equipped with full secondary containment systems and the cabinet or locker would need to be situated on a concrete pad with curbs and without accessible floor drains. This would provide additional containment in the event of a release. There are also inspection requirements for greater than 10-day storage facilities that would increase the probability that a leaking container would be identified and remediated. However, the potential quantity of waste stored at permitted storage facility is greater than that for a less than 10-day transfer station. The potential for impacts to surface water from storage or accidental release of hazardous wastes are unlikely for the indoor storage scenario for both a transfer station and for a permitted storage facility, however the likelihood of such release would be lower for a permitted storage facility than for a transfer station.

Outdoor Storage Scenario

Outdoor storage units that are not permitted RCRA storage facilities would be equipped with spill containment systems in accordance with NFPA Codes and OSHA requirements such that liquid releases would be contained within the unit. It is not likely that storage area itself would be equipped with a full secondary containment system unless the storage unit were a RCRA permitted storage facility, however, the DOJ COPS Office anticipates that the storage cabinets and lockers would provide containment of releases within the cabinets and lockers. Outdoor storage facilities that are RCRA permitted storage facilities are required to have full secondary containment systems to contain liquid releases, including storm water runoff. Therefore, liquid releases occurring at outdoor storage facility that is a permitted RCRA hazardous waste storage facility would be less likely to migrate to a nearby surface water body directly or through contact with storm water runoff. There are also inspection requirements for greater than 10-day storage facilities that increase the probability that a leaking container would be identified and remediated. The potential for impacts to surface water from storage or accidental release of hazardous wastes are unlikely for the outdoor storage scenario for both a transfer station and for a permitted RCRA hazardous waste storage facility, however the likelihood of such release would be lower for a RCRA permitted storage facility than for a transfer station.

A release of hazardous waste to surface water from an outdoor storage unit would have lower consequences than would an uncontrolled release resulting from a transportation accident. The DOJ COPS Office assumes that the storage units would not be located in the immediate vicinity of a river or stream and that hazardous waste released (if in the unlikely case that is not contained and controlled) would migrate to surface water by means of storm water runoff. This would dilute the release to some extent and therefore the release would likely not result in exceedance of water quality criteria. Also, this release pathway would only apply to releases of liquid waste. The DOJ COPS Office assumes that any release of a hazardous solid waste (e.g., iodine crystals) from an outdoor storage unit would be remediated prior to any significant transport of the hazardous waste away from the property.

Other Grant Funded Activities

Grant-funded training could potentially result in releases to surface water. Several states use DOJ COPS Office funding for laboratory demonstrations of the chemical production of methamphetamine to familiarize qualified law enforcement personnel with the process. Liquid wastes may also be generated during demonstration of equipment used for chemical decontamination of personnel. It is assumed that any hazardous waste generated during the demonstrations would be disposed according to federal, state, and local requirements, and would not be disposed of through drain systems. Any liquid effluents that are classified as hazardous waste are anticipated to be handled and disposed of as laboratory waste, and any liquid effluents that are classified as non-hazardous waste could be discharged to drain systems. Discharges to drain systems resulting from training activities would likely be treated in a POTW. The DOJ COPS Office does not anticipate that there would be any significant water quality impacts associated with grant-funded training.

The DOJ COPS Office Methamphetamine Initiative also may result in increased wastewater discharges from chemical analytical laboratories. These analytical laboratories process evidence from seized clandestine methamphetamine laboratories. Grants are used to purchase additional analytic equipment such as scanning electron microscopes and general laboratory supplies such as glassware and chemical analytical reagents. Grants may also fund the training of additional analytical chemists.

Typical wastewater emissions from an analytical laboratory are not anticipated to significantly affect water quality. The DOJ COPS Office anticipates that grant-funded chemical analytical laboratory activities would result in an incremental increase in the generation of wastewater, which would be managed in accordance with federal, state and local regulations, i.e., it would discharged to a POTW and would not represent a significant load with respect to the overall flow to the POTW. The DOJ COPS Office assumes that hazardous wastes generated chemical analytical laboratory operations are not disposed of through the drain system. As discussed above, DOJ COPS Office grants would only provide equipment, supplies, and personnel, not funding for construction or modification. Any new construction or modification of a chemical analytical laboratory would be subject to site-specific NEPA analysis and is outside the scope of the Proposed Action.

8.1.3   Soil Quality

Hazardous Waste Management Activities

Removal Action Scenario

Potential benefits to soil quality are anticipated from the normal conduct of removal actions under the DOJ COPS Office Methamphetamine Initiative. Clandestine drug laboratories represent a potential source of releases to surface soils from hazardous wastes stored and used at the sites. Conduct of grant-funded removal actions would reduce potential sources of releases to surface soils, including illicit discharges of hazardous waste to outdoor areas. The DOJ COPS Office does not anticipate that there would be any discharges to soil from the normal conduct of hazardous waste removal actions.

Single Family House Scenario / Rural Open Air Setting Scenario

An accidental release during a removal action conducted in an outdoor environment has the potential to affect soil quality. Such a release could occur as a result of a materials handling accident or container failure. The DOJ COPS Office considers the probability of such an occurrence to be low, however, the potential consequences of such a release could be significant if the release is not controlled. The detailed methodology and assumptions for determining soil quality impacts associated with normal operations and accidental releases to surface water are provided in Appendix M, Methodology for Assessing Soil Quality Impacts.

For a screening analysis of potential soil quality impacts for the release scenarios, the DOJ COPS Office assumed that a release of hazardous waste to soils could occur as a result of container breach or materials handling accident. The DOJ COPS Office compared the calculated soil concentration for each hazardous waste to the SSL for soil ingestion, as shown in Table 8.1-4.

Table 8.1-4
Soil Quality Impacts for the Removal Action Scenarios

Hazardous Waste Released	Release Amount (Kilograms)	Soil Ingestion SSL (mg/kg soil)	Concentration (mg/kg soil)	Percent of SSL
Toluene	100	16000	66667	416%
Acetone	100	7800	66667	854%
Sodium Dichromate	2.5	390	331	84%

Note: Soil Ingestion SSL and Calculated Soil Concentration are for Chromium+6 for Sodium Dichromate

As shown, concentrations of hazardous waste released to surface soil for the release scenarios could exceed generic SSLs by nearly a factor of ten for acetone and nearly a factor of five for toluene. Concentrations of sodium dichromate (calculated as chromium+6) are estimated to be approximately equal to the SSL. Ingestion of contaminated soils at such concentrations could represent a human exposure risk, particularly to children, and existence of contaminated soils at such concentrations would warrant remediation of the contamination.

Ingestion of contaminated soils at such concentrations could represent a human exposure risk, particularly to children, and existence of contaminated soils at such concentrations would warrant remediation of the contamination. Soil quality impacts from the release scenarios (i.e., hazardous waste releases) are assumed not to be ongoing. The DOJ COPS Office assumes that releases to soil that occur as a result of removal actions would be subject to emergency response and that therefore potential releases to soils would not represent an ongoing impact to soil quality.

Multi-unit Residential Property Scenario

The location for the Multi-unit Residential Property Scenario is assumed not to be in the vicinity of surface soils

Transportation Scenario

No significant discharges to surface soils are anticipated for normal conduct of hazardous waste transportation under the DOJ COPS Office Methamphetamine Initiative. However, a release of hazardous waste to surface soils resulting from a transportation accident has the potential to affect soil quality. The methodology and assumptions used in screening soil quality impacts for the transportation scenario are identical to those used for the removal action scenarios and are summarized in Appendix M, Methodology for Assessing Soil Quality Impacts and Table 8.1-4.

Storage Scenarios

The DOJ COPS Office does not anticipate any significant potential for releases to surface soils resulting from indoor storage. Environmental impacts to surface soils from storage or accidental release of hazardous wastes are unlikely for the outdoor storage scenario for both a transfer station and for a permitted RCRA hazardous waste storage facility, however the likelihood of such release would be lower for a RCRA permitted storage facility than for a transfer station.

Hazardous Waste Disposal

The DOJ COPS Office anticipates that disposal of hazardous wastes generated from grant-funded removal actions in RCRA Subtitle C-permitted facilities would not result in significant environmental impacts. In general, the types of hazardous wastes generated from removal actions, including flammable and combustible wastes, reactive wastes (oxidizers) and corrosive wastes (acids, bases) would be treated prior to disposal, or, in the case of flammable or combustible wastes, burned for energy recovery. Also, RCRA land disposal restrictions (LDRs) prohibit the disposal of free liquids and other untreated hazardous wastes in hazardous waste landfills. Therefore, the DOJ COPS Office does not anticipate that any untreated hazardous wastes generated from grant-funded activities would be disposed of in landfills.

DEA contractors are required to dispose of all hazardous wastes generated from removal actions in RCRA-permitted TSDFs. CESQGs may, in some states, dispose of CESQG-generated hazardous waste in non-RCRA permitted facilities, as discussed in Section 6.6. Non-RCRA permitted disposal facilities (generally state-permitted facilities) permitted to accept CESQG hazardous waste may be subject to less extensive monitoring and controls and treatment requirements than RCRA-permitted facilities and may therefore represent a somewhat higher potential for releases than RCRA-permitted facilities.

The DOJ COPS Office anticipates that treatment and disposal of treated hazardous wastes generated from grant-funded removal actions would result in minimal environmental impacts. The quantity of hazardous wastes generated from grant-funded activities is anticipated to be minimal as compared to the general throughput of hazardous waste to the RCRA-permitted TSDFs utilized by grantees. Therefore the contribution of such wastes to TSDF effluents would be minimal under most circumstances. Also, RCRA-permitted TSDFs are extensively monitored with respect to potential for environmental impacts, and TSDFs are required to implement effluent monitoring, inspection, and maintenance plans and closure and post-closure monitoring plans. Permitting of TSDFs (including renewal of permits for existing facilities) generally involves environmental and human health risk assessment, in many cases TSDFs are subject to environmental impact assessment under "little NEPAs" (e.g., under the California Environmental Quality Act. Therefore, the DOJ COPS Office concludes that the potential for environmental impact from treatment and disposal of hazardous wastes generated by grant-funded activities in minimal.

Other Grant-funded Activities

The DOJ COPS Office does not anticipate impacts to soil quality from other grant-funded activities

8.1.4   Human Health and Safety

Clandestine Drug Laboratory Seizure Activities

Clandestine drug laboratory seizure operations and removal actions present potential occupational health and safety hazards to qualified law enforcement personnel, particularly to investigative and other personnel who are first responders to clandestine drug laboratory sites. These sites generally contain hazardous materials and potentially hazardous indoor air concentrations of air contaminants that could result in short-term or long-term health effects to exposed individuals. These sites may also contain corrosive, flammable, or explosive materials, including booby traps, which may represent physical hazards to responders. First responders who discover clandestine drug laboratories may be entering situations where the locations and characteristics of such hazards are not well characterized. Personnel would characterize, package, label, mark, and physically remove hazardous wastes from the clandestine drug laboratory locations. These activities have the potential to result in occupational exposure to improperly stored hazardous wastes and to other physical and chemical hazards that may not have been discovered during conduct of law enforcement activities. Even considering the wider availability of personal protective equipment, state and local law enforcement agencies may not necessarily be able to afford to purchase and maintain the types of personal protective equipment (PPE) for clandestine drug laboratory seizures. [50] [51]

The Centers for Disease Control (CDC) Agency for Toxic Substances and Disease Registry (ATSDR) maintains the Hazardous Substances Emergency Events Surveillance (HSEES) System to collect and analyze information about hazardous substance release events, including events occurring at clandestine methamphetamine laboratories. The CDC reported that in 1999 three police officers in Iowa suffered respiratory irritation after exposure to anhydrous ammonia and ether emissions during seizure of a residential clandestine methamphetamine laboratory. The police officers required decontamination at the site and treatment at a local hospital. [52] The CDC also reported that of 67 injured first responders (including 55 police officers) reported by state health departments in Iowa, Minnesota, Missouri, Oregon, and Washington, 57 were not wearing personal protective equipment at the time of injury, including 45 police officers. Approximately one-third of the 36 reported injury events involved exposure to anhydrous ammonia and one-third involved exposure to hydrochloric acid. [53] Seven of the reported events involved explosions. Approximately two-thirds of reported injuries to police officers involved respiratory irritation. The ATSDR reported that one of the agency's health investigators conducting environmental sampling at an inactive residential clandestine methamphetamine laboratory experienced second-degree chemical burns from acid encountered while conducting sampling activities at the site. [54]

The ATSDR and medical department and health researchers have reported on chemical hazards related to methamphetamine laboratories, and reported that law enforcement officers have been exposed to respiratory and other hazards and injured while serving warrants and conducting investigations of clandestine drug laboratory activities, and also reported that prior to the recent wider availability of personal protective equipment, law

---

[50] Hughart, J., 2000. Chemical Hazards Related to Clandestine Drug Laboratories, Agency for Toxic Substances and Disease Registry, 2000.

[51] Chesley, Dr. Michelle R., 1999. Methamphetamines: An Epidemic of Clandestine Labs and Health Risk. Howard University Hospital, Department of Emergency Medicine, Washington DC, September 28, 1999.

[52] CDC, 2000. Public Health Consequences Among First Responders to Emergency Events Associated With Illicit Methamphetamine Laboratories – Selected States, 1996 – 1999. U.S. Centers for Disease Control, Morbidity and Mortality Weekly Report, November 17, 2000.

[53] CDC, 2000. Public Health Consequences Among First Responders to Emergency Events Associated With Illicit Methamphetamine Laboratories – Selected States, 1996 – 1999. U.S. Centers for Disease Control, Morbidity and Mortality Weekly Report, November 17, 2000.

[54] Hughart, J., 2000. Chemical Hazards Related to Clandestine Drug Laboratories, Agency for Toxic Substances and Disease Registry, 2000.

enforcement officers conducting clandestine drug laboratory seizures have experienced both acute and chronic health effects. Even considering the wider availability of personal protective equipment, state and local law enforcement agencies may not necessarily be able to afford to purchase and maintain the types of personal protective equipment for clandestine drug laboratory seizures. [55] [56]

The EPA has published a fact sheet concerning hazards associated with clandestine methamphetamine laboratories, particular with respect to illicit theft and storage of anhydrous ammonia. [57] The EPA indicates that ammonia's low boiling point, affinity for water, and inhalation hazard, may result in responders being injured if not wearing appropriate PPE. The use of self-contained positive-pressure breathing apparatus is appropriate during a response to an anhydrous ammonia release, and cryogenic gloves with a moisture barrier may also be needed to protect against freezing and/or chemical burns.

The Proposed Action is anticipated to result in health and safety benefits and overall decrease the potential for occupational exposure of qualified law enforcement personnel to hazards associated with clandestine drug laboratory seizures. The increased availability of grant-funded personnel training, personal protective equipment for law enforcement personnel, and environmental monitoring equipment for use in assessing laboratory site hazards is anticipated to significantly reduce the potential for occupational exposure of law enforcement personnel participating in laboratory seizures and associated removal actions. However, some potential hazards could result from increased law enforcement activities. When more laboratories are seized, agents are spending more labor hours during removal actions in the vicinity of clandestine methamphetamine laboratory hazards. This could result in increased incidence of exposure to laboratory hazards such as hazardous waste, and booby traps such as explosives. This potential for heightened incidence of exposure is balanced by the increased availability of safety equipment to allow law enforcement personnel to better identify and protect against these hazards.

The Proposed Action is also anticipated to increase awareness of health and safety hazards of clandestine drug laboratory operations and result in an increase in the number of seizures of clandestine drug laboratories conducted by grant-funded personnel. For example, law enforcement agents that receive comprehensive training in clandestine methamphetamine laboratory enforcement, drug recognition, drug symptomology, and chemical analysis could perform more aspects of methamphetamine law enforcement. Grant-funded overtime potentially could result in an increased number of laboratory seizures, and decreases in production/distribution of methamphetamine. Grant-supported analyses of clandestine laboratory hazards could reduce the exposure of occupants and

---

[55] Hughart, J., 2000. Chemical Hazards Related to Clandestine Drug Laboratories, Agency for Toxic Substances and Disease Registry, 2000.
[56] Chesley, Dr. Michelle R., 1999. Methamphetamines: An Epidemic of Clandestine Labs and Health Risk. Howard University Hospital, Department of Emergency Medicine, Washington DC, September 28, 1999.
[57] EPA, 2000. Anhydrous Ammonia Theft, United States Environmental Protection Agency, Office of Solid Waste and Emergency Response, (5104), EPA Publication Number EPA-F-00-005, March 2000, http://www.epa.gov/ceppo/pubs/csalert.pdf

neighbors, including children. In addition, grant-funded analytic laboratory chemists and equipment should facilitate the analyses of evidence. Grant-funded education/outreach increases public awareness of health and safety hazards.

The DOJ COPS Office Initiative grants allow law enforcement agencies to purchase personal protective equipment and safety equipment to protect law enforcement officials from potential health and safety impacts. In addition, potential human health and safety benefits would result with respect to public safety. Specifically, the Iowa State methamphetamine initiative uses grants to purchase locking caps for ammonia storage tanks on farms. The locks deter thieves from removing ammonia to use for processing methamphetamine. Many states use grant funding to purchase safety vehicles, including SUVs or other four-wheel drive vehicles in order to transport safety equipment and personnel. Better training, personal protective equipment, and better monitoring equipment obtained through the DOJ COPS Office Methamphetamine Initiative would decrease the likelihood of occupational exposure during removal actions.

Storage Scenarios

A spill of a hazardous liquid could result in a fire. Should a hazardous liquid spill and catch fire in an indoor or outdoor storage unit, the consequences of the spill and fire would depend upon the types and quantity of waste stored in the unit, the location of the unit, and timeliness of the response to the fire. Other chemicals stored in the unit (e.g., oxidizers) could become involved in the fire and thus further promote the reactivity and intensity of the fire. However, as discussed in Section 5.3, both EPA and States have standards and guidelines for storage of incompatible wastes, and such wastes may be segregated from the flammable and combustible hazardous wastes involved in any fire. It is assumed that no pressurized flammable gases are contained in the storage unit; otherwise there would be a great potential for explosion.

The rapidity of response will largely determine the degree of impact to the building and any human receptors. If the storage unit is located at a fire station, trained firefighting personnel could immediately respond to the fire. If the storage unit was located at a police station, response of trained firefighters could take longer, potentially affecting the extent and consequences of a fire. The normal functions in the building (e.g., responding to public safety/public emergencies) could be temporarily compromised by the fire; however, the DOJ COPS Office anticipates that the amount of smoke inside the building would be minimal assuming a rapid response. Assuming a rapid response, the DOJ COPS Office anticipates that the effects of a fire would be limited and contained by responders.

The DOJ COPS Office anticipates that the fire and smoke from either an indoor or outdoor fire would not likely compromise the normal functions of the building. After an indoor fire, the interior of the building may have to be decontaminated. Decontamination may make parts of the building unavailable for use for a short period of time. For an outdoor storage unit fire, the extent of damage to the building would depend upon the location of the storage unit in relation to the building. Assuming a rapid response, the DOJ COPS Office anticipates that the effects of a fire would be limited and contained by responders.

Indoor Storage Scenario

A fire in an indoor storage unit could initially be limited to the storage unit. Standards for location of indoor storage units are summarized in Section 5.3. Storage units may or may not be equipped with fire suppression systems (see Section 5.3). The DOJ COPS Office assumes that storage units would be designed and sited in accordance with fire protection codes (e.g., NFPA Code 30) and would meet requirements outlined in grant award conditions. An indoor fire involving less than 100 kilograms (e.g., approximately 30 gallons) could be initially limited to only one storage cabinet or locker. The storage unit either would be vented to the outside of the building or would not be vented. The rapidity of response will largely determine the degree of impact to the building and to the services provided by the personnel. Each storage cabinet or locker may contain up to 60 gallons of hazardous waste. If the fire occurred in a cabinet containing 60 gallons (more than 100 kilograms) of flammable liquids, the fire would involve the additional materials and the fire would likely engulf the full storage cabinet. NFPA Codes and OSHA and RCRA requirements for storage cabinet design and separation distances between other storage cabinets would help limit the potential spread of the fire (see Section 5.3). Smoke would potentially spread throughout the building. Any hazardous materials lockers would probably not be located in the same area as the flammable liquids storage cabinet. It is assumed that no pressured flammable gases are contained in the storage cabinet; otherwise there would be a great potential for explosion.

For a fire involving a full 60 gallons of flammable liquids, the rapidity of fire response will largely determine the degree of impact to the building and the services provided by the building personnel. If the storage cabinet was located in a fire station, trained firefighting personnel could immediately respond to the fire. If the storage cabinet is located in a police station, response of trained firefighters could take longer, potentially affecting the extent and consequences of a fire. The normal functions in the building (e.g., responding to public safety/public emergencies) could be temporarily compromised by fire and smoke and subsequent need for decontamination. The DOJ COPS Office assumes that the occupied structures may be 50 feet from the storage unit. Smoke generated by the fire could therefore require that adjoining residential or commercial areas be evacuated.

Outdoor Storage Scenario

The impacts of a fire in a storage unit located outdoors would depend on the location of the storage unit in relation to the building. Standards for location of outdoor storage units are summarized in Section 5.3. A fire could initially be limited to the storage area. Additional chemicals stored in the unit, if not segregated, could become involved in the fire and thus further promote the reactivity and intensity of the fire. For an outdoor fire involving between 100 and 1,000 kilograms of hazardous material, it is likely If more than one storage locker becomes involved in a fire, the fire could involving more than 100 kilograms of flammable liquids. In this case the fire would intensify and smoke generated by the fire could necessitate evacuation of adjacent buildings. The rapidity of response will largely determine the degree of impact to the building and to the services provided by the personnel. The DOJ COPS Office anticipates that for the outdoor fire scenario the normal functions of the building would not likely be extensively compromised by fire and smoke, and the building would probably not be damaged.

Other Grant-funded Activities

The Proposed Action is anticipated to have health and safety benefits to the general public as well as to law enforcement personnel. Some states have used grant funding to administer drug and chemical diversion programs. These programs focus on investigating the illegal distribution and use of legitimate narcotics by those licensed to handle drugs such as doctors, dentists, veterinarians, and nurses. Drug diversion agents monitor legal vendors or owners of methamphetamine precursor materials (such as denatured alcohol and anhydrous ammonia). In some states, drug diversion agents provided farms with locks for anhydrous ammonia tanks (the ammonia is used for fertilizers on farms). Agents also track drug theft, forgery, and wire fraud cases to determine if legitimate narcotics are being diverted to illegitimate uses. The potential reduction in the number of clandestine drug laboratories could result in benefits to public health and safety due to increased law enforcement activities. In addition, the DOJ COPS Office Methamphetamine Initiative supports state and local Drug Endangered Children programs, discussed in Section 9.0.

8.1.6 Social Effects

Hazardous Waste Management Activities

Storage Scenarios

The DOJ COPS Office Methamphetamine Initiative has potential social impacts related to the potential for temporary loss of use of building areas of a police or fire station or other government property the event of a fire, release, or other accident involving hazardous waste in an indoor storage unit. In the event of a fire or other accident event, areas of the building may need to be evacuated, and building areas could require decontamination before the areas may be reoccupied. Decontamination could require several days to complete. Also, the storage unit itself, presumably damaged by the fire or other accident event, would have to be replaced. Potential temporary loss of use of building areas resulting from a fire or other accident event represents a potential social and economic cost to police/fire station, and could interfere with the function of the police/fire station as a whole or interfere with the implementation of the methamphetamine initiative.

No substantive potential social impacts related to the potential temporary loss of use of DEA contractor property are associated with DOJ COPS Office Methamphetamine Initiative. Potential temporary loss of use of building areas of DEA contractor-operated transfer stations could result from a fire, release, or other accident involving hazardous waste stored at the transfer station. Such temporary loss of use of property would represent a business cost to the DEA contractor, however the DOJ COPS Office does not anticipate that any such loss would interfere significantly interfere with the ability of DEA contractors to conduct removal actions. The DOJ COPS Office anticipates that in the event of temporary loss of use of property the DEA contractor would have the ability to divert hazardous waste shipments from clandestine drug laboratories to another DEA contractor-operated transfer station until the use of the property is restored.

The potential for diversion of hazardous wastes, and associated social effects of such diversion, could occur at a local police or fire station under the DOJ COPS Office Methamphetamine Initiative. State and local qualified law enforcement personnel and other persons that may have access to facilities where storage units are located would not be subject to background checks and clearances, and therefore there would be less opportunity for screening and limiting the number of individuals that would have access to the areas where hazardous waste is handled and stored. Although personnel participating in a law enforcement program would not be expected to present a risk of diversion, the police stations and fire stations where storage units may be situated could also be accessible by non-program persons, including non-government personnel and members of the public, which could increase the risk of diversion particularly if the storage unit is located outdoors. Security requirements for storage unit locations for DEA contractors exceed regulatory requirements, and security requirements for storage units operated by grantees are not anticipated to be as stringent as those required for DEA contractors under the provisions of the DEA contracts. The DOJ COPS Office anticipates that grantees may or may not implement security measures for their storage units that are as stringent as for DEA contractors. This could increase the potential that hazardous wastes could be diverted from the storage unit location as compared to storage units operated by DEA contractors.

Other Grant Funded Activities

The DOJ COPS Office Methamphetamine Initiative is anticipated to result in social benefits to communities where clandestine drug laboratories are being operated. General increased funding for state and local law enforcement agencies would result in greater social benefits through improvement in the quality, scope, quantity of law enforcement activities. Grant-funded overtime potentially could result in an increased number of laboratory seizures, and decreases in production/distribution of methamphetamine. Grant-supported analyses of clandestine laboratory hazards could reduce the exposure of occupants and neighbors, including children. In addition, grant-funded analytic laboratory chemists and equipment should facilitate the analyses of evidence and prosecution of suspects. An increased number of clandestine methamphetamine laboratory seizures with associated reductions in the production and distribution of drugs would result in a social benefit under the DOJ COPS Office Methamphetamine Initiative.

8.2   No Action Alternative

This section describes the environmental consequences analyses for the No Action Alternative. Under the No Action Alternative, the DOJ COPS Office Methamphetamine Initiative would not receive Federal funding, and no funding would be dispersed by the

DOJ COPS Office to prospective grantees. Therefore, no grant-funded activities would be conducted under the No Action Alternative.

Under the No Action Alternative, it is assumed that loss of funding for the DOJ COPS Office Methamphetamine Initiative would result in a reduction in the effectiveness of state and local law enforcement activities related to state and local methamphetamine initiatives. Under the No Action Alternative, law enforcement activities and equipment purchases proposed for grant funding would not be funded. Law enforcement agencies that requested grant funding would either forgo such activities and purchases due to lack of such funding, or would redirect funding for such activities and purchases from other areas of their state and local budgets. The DOJ COPS Office cannot predict how each state or local law enforcement agency would react to a loss of methamphetamine initiative grant funding, however, the DOJ COPS Office assumes that state and local governments would not be able to replace a significant amount of the Federal grant funding with state and local funding. The DOJ COPS Office Grant Award Conditions require that grant funding not be used to supplant existing funding. Budget Narratives prepared by prospective grantees for FY2002 generally explicitly indicate that requested federal funding could not be replaced by state or local budget resources. The DOJ COPS Office therefore assumes that fewer law enforcement personnel would be deployed and less equipment would be available for state and local methamphetamine initiatives, and that as a result the effectiveness of such initiatives would be reduced.

The DOJ COPS Office assumes that under the No Action Alternative fewer clandestine drug laboratories may be seized, as a result of the elimination of grant funding for state and local law enforcement activities and loss of availability of regular and overtime personnel and equipment. However, the DOJ COPS Office cannot predict whether, where, or to what extent, a reduction in the number of clandestine drug laboratories seizures would occur under the No Action Alternative, as this would be affected by state and local agency decisions concerning how to respond to the loss of grant funding.

Under the No Action Alternative, DEA contractors under the DEA National Clandestine Laboratory Cleanup Program would not receive Federal funding to manage hazardous waste generated from clandestine drug laboratory seizures conducted by state or local law enforcement agencies. State and local agencies would be responsible for securing alternative sources of funding to conduct hazardous waste management activities related to clandestine drug laboratory seizures. Therefore, drugs, drug precursors, and/or hazardous waste may remain in place at clandestine drug laboratory locations for an unspecified period of time until such time as alternative sources of funding are identified.

8.2.1 Air Quality

The No Action Alternative would not result in any reduction in baseline air quality impacts that are assumed to be resulting from releases from improperly stored hazardous wastes at clandestine drug laboratory locations. Clandestine drug laboratories that are not identified and seized due to resource constraints would represent a potential continuing impact to air quality with respect to air emissions from methamphetamine cooking operations and from fugitive emissions and illicit disposal of hazardous wastes from such operations. The potential for exposure to air emissions would continue to exists with respect to occupants of the clandestine drug laboratory and adjacent properties.

Hazardous wastes remaining in place under the No Action Alternative would represent a continuing hazard with respect to potential accidental releases to air. In the event that 100 kilograms of ammonia were released inside an apartment (15,000 cubic feet) in a multi-unit residential property (e.g., resulting from failure of a container), the anticipated ammonia concentration initially would be 320,000 parts per million (ppm). This would cause fatalities for anyone entering the apartment and becoming exposed to the ammonia gas. Adjacent apartment units could be expected to have ammonia concentrations of approximately 6,400 ppm, far exceeding the ERPG-2 level of 150 ppm, and exposure to such concentration would impair the ability of persons to take protective action. As a result, persons in adjacent apartments would experience severe health effects.

8.2.2   Water and Soil Quality

Clandestine drug laboratories that are not identified and seized as a result of resource constraints would represent a potential continuing impact to water quality with respect to illicit disposal of hazardous wastes to sinks, bathtubs, or toilets, which could potentially affect the operation of POTWs or contaminate domestic septic systems. Illicit disposal of hazardous wastes outdoors (single family home backyards, rural areas) could result in surface water and surface soil contamination. Hazardous wastes remaining in place under the No Action Alternative would represent a continuing potential for impacts to surface water and soil quality with respect to potential accidental releases to surface water and surface soils. Under the Proposed Action, the DOJ COPS Office has assumed that accidental releases to surface water or surface soils resulting from hazardous waste management activities would be remediated by personnel conducting the activities. However, under the No Action Alternative, in the event of an accidental release (e.g., resulting from a container failure) resulting soil or surface water would not be remediated in a timely manner and would represent a continuing impact to surface water and soils.

8.2.3   Human Health and Safety

Under the No Action Alternative, no grant-funded activities would be conducted. This would involve a reduction in the availability of regular and overtime personnel, law enforcement systems and equipment (surveillance equipment, computers, etc.) safety equipment (personal protective equipment, on-site environmental monitoring equipment, etc.) and a reduction in the availability of qualified law enforcement personnel health and safety training. This could potentially increase the likelihood of occupational exposure to law enforcement personnel and the public to chemical and physical hazards. Grant funding for law enforcement equipment has been requested by state and local methamphetamine initiatives in response to specific law enforcement needs of their initiatives. For example, initiatives in Mississippi and Utah requested funding for off road vehicles and safety equipment trailers to enable law enforcement officers to travel to and seize clandestine drug laboratories that are frequently located in remote areas of their states. Such state/local initiative-specific needs would not be met under the No Action Alternative.

Continued operation of clandestine drug laboratories that are not identified and seized as a result of resource constraints would represent a continued health and safety hazard to the public. Reduced availability of equipment for on site monitoring of environmental and physical hazards for non-grant funded clandestine drug laboratory seizure operations could result in potential occupational exposure of law enforcement personnel. Grant funding for specific environmental monitoring equipment have been requested by state and local methamphetamine initiatives in response to specific hazards identified by those initiatives. For example, the Oregon and Wisconsin initiatives have identified an increase in the incidence of explosive devices found at clandestine drug laboratories, and requested grant funding for specialized equipment to respond to this identified hazard. Such state/local initiative-specific needs would not be met under the No Action Alternative.

Reduction in the availability of training also represents a potential impact to health and safety. Qualified law enforcement personnel would not be permitted to use Air Purifying Respirators (APR) or Self-contained Breathing Apparatus (SCBA) equipment unless they receive the training to do so, even if the equipment itself is available, and would not be able to perform certain activities at clandestine drug laboratory sites without OSHA health and safety training. Qualified law enforcement personnel also would not become as familiar with the specific types of chemical and physical hazards that are associated with clandestine drug laboratories without receiving specialized training. The reduction in the availability of training under the No Action Alternative would therefore result in a reduction of the capability of law enforcement personnel to identify and respond to specific health and safety hazards associated with clandestine drug laboratory sites.

Under the No Action Alternative, drugs, drug precursors, and/or hazardous waste may remain in place at clandestine drug laboratory locations for an unspecified period of time. This would present a relatively high potential for human health exposure and safety issues for residents of the property and adjacent properties. Collocation of incompatible hazardous waste at the site may result in ignition, and could result in a building fire and in ignition or explosion of other hazardous waste containers in the unit. Residents of the property, residents of adjacent properties, and emergency responders could be exposed to air pollutants resulting from combustion of the hazardous wastes and hazards associated with exploding containers. Building fires fed by flammable hazardous wastes such as acetone or toluene could rapidly become uncontrolled and result in extensive damage to the building and potentially result in the injury or death of the building occupants if the fire becomes uncontrolled.

Potential impacts from drugs, drug precursors, and improperly stored hazardous waste also include potential human health impacts from exposure to corrosive, toxic, or reactive materials and potential safety impacts from fire or explosion. The DOJ COPS Office anticipates that containers remaining on site may not have identifying labels and may not be secured, and therefore individuals may be unaware of the hazards associated with the wastes. Persons may attempt to remove hazardous wastes or contaminated apparatus from the location for various reasons (e.g., in order to prepare the location to be reoccupied.) These persons may not have proper training and personnel protective equipment, and may breach a container or otherwise be exposed to hazards. Direct exposure of an individual to hazardous wastes in quantities anticipated to remain on site could result in severe injury or death. Also, if the property is left unsecured, improperly stored hazardous wastes, drugs, or drug precursors could result in child endangerment, as these materials would be potentially accessible and attractive to children residing at the property or in the vicinity.

If flammable hazardous waste inside a clandestine drug laboratory building caught fire, the building would be engulfed in flames and smoke. Other hazardous wastes present in the building could further promote the reactivity and intensity of the fire. The damage to the property would depend most importantly on the construction materials of the building (wood/concrete). Other factors include the fire load in the building, the rapidness of response and the ventilation condition, and the fire fighting techniques employed. Assuming a modern concrete multi-unit residential property, a response time of several minutes, and a modest degree of fire load, the fire would engulf the apartment and seriously threaten apartments on same floor and apartments below and above the fire floor. There could be fatalities/injuries for residents of adjacent apartments. The entire apartment building and perhaps nearby areas would probably need to be evacuated because of smoke and fire. There would be extensive smoke and water damage so that residents would not return to the property until such damage was repaired.

8.2.4   Social Effects

Under the No Action Alternative fewer clandestine drug laboratory seizures would be conducted. The social effects of a reduction in clandestine drug laboratory seizures include continued operation of laboratories that are not seized, and production and distribution of controlled substances from such laboratories. This has the potential to preclude the productive reuse of the property, resulting in economic impacts and potential temporary or permanent displacement of persons living at or in the vicinity of the clandestine drug laboratory. Also, there is the potential for diversion of drugs, drug precursors, other raw materials, and apparatus from clandestine drug laboratory locations under the No Action Alternative because such materials would not be removed or secured at other locations under the No Action Alternative.

9.0   Potential Impacts to Children

In accordance with Executive Order 13045, *Protection of Children From Environmental Health Risks and Safety Risks*, the DOJ COPS Office evaluated the projected effects of the Proposed Action and the No Action Alternative. The DOJ COPS Office determined that the DOJ COPS Office Methamphetamine Initiative does not create disproportionate impacts to children, but that the No Action Alternative has the potential to create disproportionate environmental health risks or safety risks to children.

Potential releases of hazardous wastes to air could potentially result from an accident during conduct of a grant-funded activity, including removal, transportation, or storage of hazardous waste. However, in the event of a release to air, the level of exposure to the released hazardous wastes via inhalation is anticipated to be greater for children than for adults because children have higher inhalation rates per unit body weight than adults. Thus, for the ammonia release scenario for the DOJ COPS Office Methamphetamine Initiative described in Section 8.1.1, children would show symptoms of respiratory irritation at lower exposure concentrations and at greater distances from the point of release than would adults. However, ERPG-2 levels specific to children are not available. Therefore, no quantitative analyses specific to children are included in the Environmental Assessment related to accidental release exposure. The DOJ COPS Office does not anticipate any disproportionate impacts to children with respect to the number of potentially exposed individuals because children are no more or less likely to be situated in the vicinity of an accidental release location than are adults. The DOJ COPS Office considers accidental releases related to grant-funded activities to be unlikely, and children would not be disproportionately subjected to the incidence of such releases, as compared to adults.

The more significant potential for disproportionate impacts to children is from the No Action Alternative. For the No Action Alternative, it is assumed that the loss of funding for the DOJ COPS Office Methamphetamine Initiative would result in a reduction in the effectiveness of state and local law enforcement activities related to methamphetamine initiatives. Under the No Action Alternative, law enforcement activities and equipment purchases proposed for grant funding would not be funded and state and local law enforcement agencies would either forgo such activities and purchases, or would redirect funding for such activities and purchases from other areas of their state and local methamphetamine initiative budgets. The DOJ COPS Office cannot predict whether, where, or to what extent, a reduction in the number of clandestine drug laboratories seizures would occur under the No Action Alternative. However, in the event that reductions in clandestine drug laboratory seizures do occur as a result of implementation of the No Action Alternative, there could be disproportionate human health and safety impacts to children.

DEA has collected data concerning exposure of children at clandestine drug laboratory locations. The number of children present at seized clandestine drug laboratory sites increased from 950 in 1999 to 2,028 in 2001, according to the DEA EPIC National Clandestine Drug Laboratory Seizure System. In 2001 approximately 700 (35 percent) of the 2,028 children tested positive for toxic levels of chemicals in their bodies. The states reporting the highest number of children present at clandestine drug laboratory sites in 2001 were California (503), Washington (326), Oregon (241), and Missouri (161), all states that receive a significant amount of earmarked grant funding under the DOJ COPS Office Methamphetamine Initiative. These figures are recognized as underreported because many states do not keep records on children present or medically evaluate them for the presence of drugs or chemicals.[58]

Clandestine methamphetamine drug laboratories are characterized by production of drugs

---

[58] National Drug Intelligence Center Information Bulletin: Children at Risk, July 2002, Document ID 2002-L0424-001

using hazardous chemicals, which may be used and stored in the food preparation areas or other areas that are accessible to children. The methamphetamine cooking process itself represents a health and safety hazard, and waste hazardous chemicals may be disposed of in sinks, bathtubs, toilets, or outdoor areas.[59, 60] Unattended drugs, cooking apparatus, or hazardous chemicals used in drug production, or contaminated air, soil, or water resulting from illicit disposal or release of hazardous wastes associated with drug production, would all represent potential exposure pathways that could disproportionately affect children.

The potential for exposure to children is significantly greater than for adults for the No Action Alternative. In the event that fewer seizures of clandestine drug laboratories occur, some clandestine drug laboratories in which children are situated may not be discovered, and the number of children potentially exposed in such locations and the duration of such exposure could increase. Children situated in a clandestine drug laboratory location would have less judgment in keeping away from unattended drugs, cooking apparatus, and toxic, corrosive, and flammable hazardous wastes than would adults, and may in fact, consider containers and apparatus to be playthings rather than dangerous articles. Therefore, there is a greater potential for a child to become exposed to hazardous waste of drugs (e.g., by contacting or breaching a container) or potentially to start a fire than for an adult. The potential for and level of exposure through ingestion pathways would be greater for children because children have a higher hand to mouth contact than adults and are more likely to contact contaminated surfaces such as carpets, floors, and soil.

Once exposed, children may be more vulnerable than adults to drugs or toxic or corrosive wastes because of differences in absorption, excretion, and metabolism rates between children and adults. Both the acute and chronic effects of exposure would be greater for children than for adults, because a child's neurological, immunological, digestive, and other bodily systems are still developing. Also, children have a higher surface area to body weight ratio than adults so exposure through the body from liquids or gases could be more intense for children (e.g., seizures, nausea, irritation, burns).[61] A level of exposure to a toxic or corrosive waste that would cause injury to an adult could be fatal to a child. For example, exposure to relatively small amounts of iodine, on the order of 200 milligrams, has been associated with fatalities in children.[62] Thus, the No Action Alternative could result in disproportionate impacts to children.

In addition, several states use grant funding to support Drug Endangered Children programs. These programs focus on identifying and protecting children that are exposed to hazards associated with methamphetamine laboratories. Some programs, like the City

---

[59] Minnesota Department of Health, General Cleanup Guidelines for Clandestine Drug Laboratories, October 2002.

[60] Minnesota Pollution Control Agency, Environmental Problems Associated with Clandestine Drug Operations, September 2000.

[61] Ferguson, Dr. Thomas J., No Date. Overview of Medical Toxicology and Potential for Exposures to Clandestine Drug Laboratories in California: University of California, Davis Department of Internal Medicine, reprinted in Minnesota Department of Health publication Response to Clandestine Drug Labs, 2002. http://www.health.state.mn.us

[62] Chesley, Dr. Michelle R., 1999. Methamphetamines: An Epidemic of Clandestine Labs and Health Risk. Howard University Hospital, Department of Emergency Medicine, Washington D.C., September 28, 1999.

of Phoenix, Arizona, work closely with local, state, federal, and private organizations. Programs aim to develop protocols for handling drug-endangered children and to train law enforcement agents, prosecutors and social workers. Grant-funded activities also may include medical screening of children for toxicity and malnourishment, emergency and long-term foster care, and psychological treatment. Under the No Action Alternative, these programs would not receive grant funding and would not be maintained or would be limited in their ability to protect children from the hazards of illegal manufacture of methamphetamine. In some cases, state or local agencies that do not yet have Drug Endangered Children programs would not be able to apply for funding to establish such programs. Thus, disproportionate impacts to health and safety of children are anticipated under the No Action Alternative.

10.0   Energy Impacts and Irreversible and Irretrievable Commitment of Resources

The DOJ COPS Office Methamphetamine Initiative would involve irreversible and irretrievable commitment of resources related to the purchase and deployment of grant-funded law enforcement equipment and also related packaging, transportation, and storage of the hazardous wastes generated from grant-funded removal actions. Resource commitments under the DOJ COPS Office Methamphetamine Initiative include personal protective equipment and packaging materials used by hazardous waste management personnel. These materials would become contaminated by hazardous waste during use and would therefore need to be disposed as hazardous waste. Other consumable materials (e.g., office supplies) would also be purchased, used, and disposed under the DOJ COPS Office Methamphetamine Initiative. Energy resources, including gasoline, diesel fuel, natural gas, and electricity, would be consumed in operating vehicles used in conducting grant-funded law enforcement activities and hazardous waste transportation, and in heating, cooling, and ventilating storage locations. The overall level of funding of the DOJ COPS Office Methamphetamine Initiative varies from year to year, however since 1998 approximately $223 million in earmarked and discretionary funding has been provided to state and local law enforcement agencies under the DOJ COPS Office Methamphetamine Initiative. Such resources would continue to be committed under the DOJ COPS Office Methamphetamine Initiative. DOJ COPS Office Methamphetamine Initiative funding may represent a significant percentage of overall funding for methamphetamine initiatives for certain state and local law enforcement agencies.

Participating state and local agencies may need to commit additional resources in establishing storage locations for hazardous waste recovered from grant-funded removal actions, depending upon whether the agencies choose to manage the recovered hazardous waste themselves. These resources would include the hazardous waste storage units themselves, associated fixtures, and the indoor building floor space or outdoor paved area space for the storage units, which would subsequently be unavailable for other uses. In some cases, grantees would construct new buildings for storage units. However, any new construction would be subject to site-specific NEPA analysis. The DOJ COPS Office anticipates that given the relatively small amount of hazardous waste anticipated to be stored in most storage units, the resource commitment of facility space for the storage units would not represent a significant commitment of government property. Under the No Action Alternative, no grant-funded activities would be conducted. Therefore, no grant-funded resources would be consumed under the No Action Alternative.

Recycling of hazardous materials recovered from clandestine drug laboratories has been considered. Although recycling may be beneficial from an environmental perspective, recycling has not been implemented because of law enforcement considerations and associated risks and costs that override the potential environmental and economic benefits of recycling. The DOJ COPS Office anticipates that under the DOJ COPS Office Methamphetamine Initiative, state and local law enforcement agencies conducting grant-funded removal actions would also not recycle recovered materials.
Therefore, the DOJ COPS Office anticipates that grantees would continue the current practice of direct disposal of hazardous materials discovered at clandestine drug laboratories at hazardous waste treatment and disposal facilities and would not implement a recycling program for recovered hazardous materials, except for recognized methods such as fuel blending that constitute both recycling and waste disposal methods.

11.0 Environmental Justice

The DOJ COPS Office evaluated the environmental effects of the Proposed Action in accordance with Executive Order 12898, *Federal Actions to Address Environmental Justice in Minority Populations and Low Income Populations*. Environmental justice issues would be raised if there were "disproportionate" and "high and adverse impacts" on minority or low-income populations. The DOJ COPS Office does not anticipate that there would be any disproportionate and high and adverse impacts associated with the DOJ COPS Office Methamphetamine Initiative. The DOJ COPS Office determined that there could be disproportionate and high and adverse impacts associated with the No Action Alternative.

DEA contractors conducted approximately 7,255 hazardous waste removal actions at clandestine drug laboratory locations in fiscal year 2002.[63] DEA does not have detailed demographic information concerning each clandestine drug laboratory location where removal actions have been conducted. However, based on the DEA's general experience in identifying and seizing clandestine drug laboratories, the DEA anticipates that many clandestine drug laboratories would be identified in areas of economically disadvantaged populations or minority and ethnic group populations. The DOJ COPS Office anticipates that clandestine drug laboratories seized through grant-funded activities may also occur in areas of economically disadvantaged populations or minority and ethnic group populations, although detailed demographic information is not available for grant-funded activities conducted under the DOJ COPS Office Methamphetamine Initiative. The DOJ COPS Office therefore anticipates that an increase in state and local law enforcement activities may result in environmental benefits to economically disadvantaged populations. However, the DOJ COPS Office can neither quantitatively determine the

---

[63] DEA El Paso Information Center, 2002.

demographics of the locations of prior grant-funded clandestine drug laboratory seizures nor predict the locations of future grant-funded seizures.

The DOJ COPS Office does not anticipate that the environmental consequences of the DOJ COPS Office Methamphetamine Initiative would result in high and adverse impacts to minority or low-income populations regarding the transportation of hazardous waste. The DOJ COPS Office cannot predict the transportation routes that would be used in transporting recovered hazardous waste from removal action locations to hazardous waste storage unit locations. The DOJ COPS Office also does not have demographic information concerning the personnel participating in the grant-funded activities, and cannot predict the future participation of personnel in grant-funded activities. However, the DOJ COPS Office does not anticipate that storage units would be disproportionately located in minority or low income areas, or that the personnel participating in grant-funded activities would disproportionately be members of low-income or minority groups.

Under the No Action Alternative, the DOJ COPS Office anticipates a potential reduction in the effectiveness of law enforcement activities related to methamphetamine, and anticipates that the number of clandestine drug laboratory seizures conducted by law enforcement agencies would decrease as a result of a decrease in the amount of funding available to such agencies. Clandestine drug laboratories may be disproportionately located in areas of minority or low-income populations, and therefore may disproportionately affect economically disadvantaged persons or persons of minority groups or ethnic groups. Affected individuals may include the occupants of the clandestine drug laboratories themselves (including children), maintenance workers in multi-unit residential properties that may encounter such laboratories or become exposed to hazardous waste releases from such laboratories, and neighboring residents of clandestine drug laboratory properties that are located in low-income, minority and ethnic group population areas. Any reduction in the number of clandestine drug laboratories seized would increase the potential for health and safety impacts from the operation of such laboratories. Distribution of methamphetamine from such clandestine drug laboratories may also disproportionately affect economically disadvantaged persons or persons of minority groups or ethnic groups.

12.0 Energy Impacts

Under the DOJ COPS Office Methamphetamine Initiative, minor amounts of energy in the form of gasoline, natural gas, diesel fuel, and other fossil fuels, would be consumed in conducting grant-funded activities, conducting grant-funded removal actions, and transporting hazardous wastes recovered to storage units. Minor amounts of energy, primarily in the form of electricity and natural gas, would be expended in heating, ventilating, and cooling the storage unit locations under the DOJ COPS Office Methamphetamine Initiative. The DOJ COPS Office does not anticipate that the location of storage units at existing government buildings would have a significant effect on energy consumption for those buildings. In addition, DEA contractors utilize "fuel blending" energy recovery as one disposal option for recovered hazardous wastes, where hazardous wastes with high fuel value (e.g., toluene, acetone) are used to augment the heating value of other wastes burned for energy recovery. Hazardous wastes recovered from removal actions may also be subjected to fuel blending. Therefore, depending upon the specific hazardous wastes recovered, the DOJ COPS Office Methamphetamine Initiative may have an energy benefit. There would be no energy expenditure or energy benefit for the No Action Alternative, as no grant-funded activities would be conducted.

13.0   Coastal Zone Management Act and Coastal Barrier Resources

Some clandestine drug laboratories may be located within a State's approved coastal zone management area. However, the Coastal Zone Management Act's requirements related to consistency determinations do not apply to the Proposed Action, because the Proposed Action does not involve any land use planning activity. In the event that a clandestine drug laboratory is identified and seized within a designated coastal zone management area as a result of grant-funded activities, the potential for environmental impacts to such area would be reduced as a result of cessation of the illegal operation and removal of illegally stored hazardous wastes under the DOJ COPS Office Methamphetamine Initiative. Accidental releases of hazardous wastes to surface water could occur in the conduct of grant-funded activities under the DOJ COPS Office Methamphetamine Initiative, including the removal, transportation, and storage of hazardous wastes. Any releases to surface water could result in exceedance of water quality criteria, as discussed in Section 8.1.2 and Appendix L. The DOJ COPS Office considers it unlikely that a release of hazardous waste resulting from a removal action or transportation accident would occur in the vicinity of or would affect a coastal zone management area. The DOJ COPS Office does not anticipate that under the Proposed Action hazardous waste would be stored in the vicinity of a coastal zone management area, however it is possible that storage in the vicinity of such area could occur under the Proposed Action.

Any accidental releases to surface water that occur in the conduct of grant-funded activities would be subject to emergency response, and the agency conducting the activity would be responsible for remediating any environmental contamination resulting from the release. Personnel conducting hazardous waste management activities would be trained to conduct such activities safely and would be trained to respond to release incidents. Storage unit containment systems would further reduce the potential for and consequences of releases to surface water from the Proposed Action.

Benefits and potential impacts to coastal barrier resources under the DOJ COPS Office Methamphetamine Initiative are similar to those for coastal zone management areas, described above. The No Action Alternative would not result in a reduction of potential impacts to coastal zone management areas, and would not result in any benefits to coastal zone management areas, as no grant-funded activities would be conducted under the No Action Alternative.

14.0   Historic Preservation

Based on DEA's experience, clandestine drug laboratory sites are rarely if ever found in properties listed on the National Register of Historic Places or in properties that are eligible for such listing. The DOJ COPS Office anticipates that clandestine drug laboratories identified and seized as a result of grant-funded activities would also rarely, if ever, be located in National Register listed or eligible properties. It is possible that a clandestine drug laboratory may be located in an older residential structure eligible for listing, however, it would be infeasible for law enforcement officials to determine the eligibility status of a property prior to conduct of law enforcement actions or removal actions. Removal actions do not generally result in significant property damage, although subsequent remediation of residual environmental contamination may do so. However, under the Proposed Action, the DOJ COPS Office and other law enforcement agencies are not responsible for remediation of the clandestine drug laboratory property, and historic preservation issues associated with remediation activities therefore would not be considered part of the Proposed Action.

15.0   Wild and Scenic Rivers

Clandestine drug laboratories could be located in the vicinity of a river that is included in the Wild and Scenic Rivers System or that is designated for potential addition to the system. In the event that a clandestine drug laboratory is identified and seized in the vicinity of a designated Wild and Scenic River or river designated for potential addition as a result of grant-funded activities, the potential for environmental impacts to such area would be reduced as a result of cessation of the illegal operation and removal of illegally and improperly stored hazardous wastes.

The DOJ COPS Office does not anticipate environmental consequences to wild and scenic rivers as a result of the normal conduct of grant-funded activities. The DOJ COPS Office anticipates that releases of hazardous wastes to air, water, or soil as a result of the normal conduct of removal actions, transportation, and storage of hazardous wastes would be minimal and would not affect any wild and scenic rivers in the vicinity of which such activities were conducted. The DOJ COPS Office also does not anticipate that the normal conduct of other grant-funded activities would affect any wild and scenic rivers.

Accidental releases of hazardous wastes to surface water could occur in the conduct of grant-funded activities under the DOJ COPS Office Methamphetamine Initiative. Such releases to surface water could result in exceedance of water quality criteria, as discussed in Section 8.1.2 and Appendix L. The DOJ COPS Office considers it unlikely that a release of hazardous waste resulting from a removal action or transportation accident would occur in the vicinity of or would affect a wild and scenic river. However, it is possible that such an incident could occur. The DOJ COPS Office does not anticipate that under the Proposed Action hazardous waste would be stored in the vicinity of a wild and scenic river, however it is possible that storage in the vicinity of such area could occur under the Proposed Action.

Any accidental releases to surface water that occur in the conduct of grant-funded activities, including conduct of removal actions, transportation, or storage of hazardous waste, would be subject to emergency response, and the agency conducting the activity would be responsible for remediating any environmental contamination resulting from the release. This would reduce the potential for and consequences of releases to surface water from the Proposed Action.

The No Action Alternative would not result in a reduction of potential impacts to wild and scenic rivers, and would not result in any benefits to wild and scenic rivers, as no grant-funded activities would be conducted under the No Action Alternative.

16.0 Threatened and Endangered Species

Clandestine drug laboratories could be located in the vicinity of threatened or endangered species habitat. However, it would be infeasible for law enforcement officials to determine the status of a property prior to conduct of law enforcement actions or removal actions. In the event that a clandestine drug laboratory is identified and seized in the vicinity of a threatened or endangered species habitat as a result of grant-funded activities under the DOJ COPS Office Methamphetamine Initiative, the potential for environmental impacts to such area would be reduced as a result of the cessation of the illegal operation and removal of illegally stored hazardous wastes. Operation of clandestine drug laboratories in rural settings has been found to have environmental impacts to habitat in the vicinity of the operation, including mortality of trees and other vegetation in the vicinity as a result of fugitive releases of air pollutants.[64]

The DOJ COPS Office does not anticipate environmental consequences to endangered or threatened species habitat as a result of the normal conduct of grant-funded activities. The DOJ COPS Office anticipates that releases of hazardous wastes to air, water, or soil as a result of the normal conduct of removal actions, transportation, and storage of hazardous wastes would be minimal and would not affect any endangered or threatened species habitat in which such activities were conducted. The DOJ COPS Office also does not anticipate that the conduct of other grant-funded activities would affect endangered or threatened species habitat.

The DOJ COPS Office considers it unlikely that a release of hazardous waste resulting from a transportation accident could occur in the vicinity of endangered or threatened species habitat. The DOJ COPS Office also does not anticipate that any storage units would be located in the vicinity of threatened or endangered species habitat, and therefore impacts to such areas are considered to be unlikely. However, it is possible that hazardous wastes could be removed, transported, or stored in the vicinity of such habitat under the Proposed Action.

In the event that an accidental release occurs in conducting a grant-funded activity, habitat in the vicinity of the release location could be affected. Hazardous waste releases

---

[64] Snell, Marilyn B., Welcome to Meth Country. Sierra Magazine, January/February 2001, reprinted in Minnesota Department of Health publication Response to Clandestine Drug Labs, 2002. http://www.health.state.mn.us

resulting from grant-funded activities could result in environmental concentrations that could affect biota. Accidental releases that occur in the conduct of grant-funded activities would be subject to emergency response, and the agency conducting the activity would be responsible for remediating any environmental contamination resulting from the release. This would reduce the potential for and consequences of releases from the Proposed Action.

The No Action Alternative would not result in a reduction of potential impacts to threatened or endangered species habitat, and would not result in any benefit to threatened or endangered species habitat, as no grant-funded activities would be conducted under the No Action Alternative.

17.0 Floodplain Management and Protection of Wetlands

The Proposed Action would not result in any conversion of floodplains or wetlands. However clandestine drug laboratories for which grant-funded seizures and removal actions are conducted could be located in the vicinity of floodplains or wetlands. In the event that a clandestine drug laboratory is identified and seized in the vicinity of a floodplain or wetland, the potential for environmental impacts to such area would be reduced as a result of cessation of the illegal operation and removal of illegal and improperly stored hazardous wastes under the DOJ COPS Office Methamphetamine Initiative.

The DOJ COPS Office does not anticipate environmental consequences to floodplains or wetlands as a result of the normal conduct of grant-funded activities. The DOJ COPS Office anticipates that releases of hazardous wastes to surface water as a result of the normal conduct of removal actions, transportation, and storage of hazardous wastes would be minimal and would not affect any floodplains or wetlands in the vicinity of which such activities were conducted. The DOJ COPS Office also does not anticipate that the normal conduct of other grant-funded activities would affect any floodplains or wetlands.

The DOJ COPS Office considers it unlikely that a release of hazardous waste resulting from a transportation accident could occur in the vicinity of wetland or floodplain. The DOJ COPS Office also does not anticipate that any storage units would be located in the vicinity of a wetland, and therefore the DOJ COPS Office considers it unlikely that impacts to such areas would occur as a result of the Proposed Action. However, it is possible that hazardous wastes could be removed, transported, or stored in the vicinity of a wetland or floodplain under the Proposed Action. The DOJ COPS Office does not anticipate that any storage units would be located in floodplains, and therefore the DOJ COPS Office does not expect that hazardous wastes would be released as a result of a flood.

In the event that an accidental release occurs in conducting a grant-funded activity, wetlands and floodplains in the vicinity of the release location could be affected. Hazardous waste releases resulting from grant-funded activities could result in environmental concentrations that could affect biota, and releases to surface water and soil could result in exceedance of water quality or soil quality criteria. Any accidental releases to air, surface water, or soil that occur in the conduct of grant-funded activities would be subject to emergency response, and the agency conducting the activity would be responsible for remediating any environmental contamination resulting from the release. This would reduce the potential for and consequences of releases from the Proposed Action.

The USGS model used to estimate water quality impacts that would result from accidental releases to surface water is based on dispersion of the release into a flowing stream or river, rather than a relatively static wetland. Therefore the peak concentrations and durations shown in Appendix L may not be representative of impacts to wetlands. Release of hazardous waste to wetlands would potentially have a higher impact than the same amount of hazardous waste released to a stream or river, because the rate of dispersion of the release would be greater in a flowing stream or river than in a wetland.

The No Action Alternative would not result in a reduction of potential impacts to wetlands or result in any benefits to wetlands, as no grant-funded activities would be conducted under the No Action Alternative.

18.0   Farmland Protection

The Proposed Action would not result in any conversion of farmland. It is possible that a clandestine drug laboratory would be found on a farm. DEA data from 2000, 2001, and 2002 (to date) indicate that approximately 12,000 of 29,000 clandestine drug laboratory removal actions were conducted in rural areas, and the DOJ COPS Office anticipates that clandestine drug laboratories identified as a result of grant-funded activities would also be located in large part in rural areas. However, the DOJ COPS Office does not anticipate that grant-funded activities would result in the conversion of farmland, although subsequent remediation of residual environmental contamination may do so. However, under the Proposed Action, the DOJ COPS Office and other law enforcement agencies are not responsible for remediation, and farmland conversion issues associated with remediation activities therefore would not be considered part of the Proposed Action.

19.0   Cumulative Impacts

Cumulative impacts are impacts of other actions that may be associated and contribute to the environmental consequences of the Proposed Action. Environmental consequences of the Proposed Action would be distributed among several thousand individual clandestine drug laboratory locations for which removal actions are conducted. The DOJ COPS Office's experience in implementing the DOJ COPS Office Methamphetamine Initiative is that the locations of clandestine drug laboratories are widely dispersed geographically, and law enforcement activities and associated removal actions associated with a specific clandestine drug laboratory location is not anticipated to affect other clandestine drug laboratory locations. The DOJ COPS Office is not aware of any other foreseeable actions on the part of the DOJ COPS Office that would affect the implementation of or the environmental consequences of the DOJ COPS Office Methamphetamine Initiative, therefore the DOJ COPS Office anticipates no cumulative impacts from other actions implemented by the DOJ COPS Office. In the event that DOJ COPS Office implements the No Action Alternative (*i.e.,* terminates grant funding) it is possible that some other federal, state, or local government entity would initiate an Action to provide grant funding to state and local law enforcement agencies to conduct law enforcement activities and conduct removal actions. However, the DOJ COPS Office cannot foresee whether or to what extent any such agencies would propose such Actions.

The DOJ COPS Office assessed the potential effects of foreseeable DOJ COPS Office and other DOJ programs and foreseeable state programs on the Proposed Action. The DOJ COPS Office did not identify any other foreseeable DOJ COPS Office or other DOJ programs that could affect the Proposed Action, and did not identify any programs that could be affected by the Proposed Action. It is possible that a state or local government could implement a methamphetamine initiative that could affect the Proposed Action, however, the DOJ COPS Office cannot foresee the implementation of any such program. In the event that a state or local government proposed to implement such a program, the DOJ COPS Office expects that the Agency would become aware of such a proposal through the Agency's normal relationship with state and local law enforcement agencies.

20.0 List of Preparers

Robert Lanza, Principal Chemical Engineer -- B.S., Chemical Engineering, Cornell University, 1980; M. Eng., Chemical Engineering, Cornell University, 1982 -- 22 years environmental consulting experience.

David E. Goldbloom-Helzner, Project Manager -- B.A., Chemistry, School of Arts and Sciences, Washington University, 1984; B.S., Engineering and Policy, School of Engineering, Washington University, 1984 – 16 years environmental consulting experience.

Audrey Slesinger, Associate – M. Sc. Geology, University of Bristol, England, 2000; B.S. Geological Sciences, Tufts University, 1998 – Three years environmental analysis experience.

Stefanie Shull, Analyst - B.S., Economics, University of Louisville, 2000 -- Two years environmental analysis experience.

Iliriana Mushkolaj, Associate - M.S. Environmental Sciences and Policy, University of Manchester & Central European University, Budapest, Hungary, 1996; M.S. Chemistry, University of Zagreb, Croatia, 1993; B.S. Chemistry, University of Prishtina, Kosova, 1990 - 5 years of environmental consulting experience.

This Page Intentionally Left Blank

Appendix A: Earmarked Grants, FY2001 and FY2002

STATE	GRANTEE	RATIONALE	YEAR	
			2001	2002
AL	Department of Public Safety	Vehicle, communications and evidence collection equipment, promotional supplies, training	X	
AR	Arkansas State Crime Laboratory	Hire three additional chemists	X	
AR	Arkansas State Police	State police training, lab equipment and supplies, training	X	
AR	Arkansas State Crime Laboratory	Vehicle, personnel costs, laboratory supplies, training		X
AR	Arkansas State Police	Laboratory equipment and supplies, safety equipment and personal protection supplies		X
AR	University of Arkansas	Training equipment and supplies, computer		X
AZ	City of Phoenix Police	Vehicle, trailer, personal protection equipment and supplies, surveillance equipment, cameras, computers, microscopes, training materials, safety equipment		X
CA	California Department of Justice, Bureau of Narcotic Enforcement	Funding for a continuation of a portion of the comprehensive CALMS program.		X
CA	Merced Police Department	Software, drug screening and chemical analysis kits, training		X
HI	State of Hawaii (Narcotics Enforcement Division)	Address methamphetamine diversion, production, distribution, and enforcement efforts.	X	
IA	Iowa Division of Narcotics	Regional Methamphetamine Training Center Audio-visual equipment, camera, computer equipment, GPS, air monitors, travel, supplies		X
IA	Governor's Office of Drug Control	Anhydrous ammonia tank locks		X
ID	Idaho State Police Headquarters	Equipment, supplies, instructors and travel for training	X	
IN	Indiana State Police Department	Waste disposal and safety processing vehicles, safety trailers, chemical analysis equipment and supplies, safety equipment, training	X	
IN	Indiana State Police Department	Processing and disposal vehicles, laboratory equipment and supplies, personal protection equipment and supplies, training equipment		X
KS	Kansas Bureau of Investigations	Combat methamphetamine and to train officers in those types of investigations	X	
KS	Kansas Bureau of Investigation	Laboratory supplies and personal protection equipment		X
KS	Riley County Police Department	Vehicle, communications and surveillance equipment and supplies		X
KS	Wichita Police Department	Vehicle, hazmat vehicle, supplies and equipment for safety, evidence, surveillance, and communications		X
KY	Davies County Sheriff's Department	Assist local enforcement agencies local in combating production and distribution of methamphetamine.	X	
LA	Ascension Parish Sheriff's Office	Support officer training and outreach programs.	X	
MO	Henry Co. Sheriff's Department	Computer and related equipment and supplies		X

State	Organization	Description		
MO	Mid-Missouri Unified Strike Team and Narcotics Group	City of Boonville - Interagency coordination, technical assistance, personnel costs		X
MO	Missouri C.O.M.E.T. program	Computer, office and communications equipment, overtime wages.		X
MO	MSSC Regional Crime Lab	Laboratory equipment and software		X
MO	NEMO Narcotics Task Force	Surveillance and communications equipment, computer, GPS, safety gear		X
MO	Newton County Sheriff's Dept. (SWMO Drug Task Force)	Overtime for officers, investigative equipment and supplies, vehicle leases, conference travel, outreach		X
MO	North Central Missouri Drug Task Force	Surveillance vehicle and equipment, office security equipment, overtime hours, community outreach		X
MO	Pemiscott Sheriff's Office	Web site development		X
MO	SEMO Drug Task Force (Mississippi County)	Overtime hours for officers, surveillance and safety equipment, training, AC unit, communications equipment, computers		X
MO	South Central Drug Task Force	Overtime hours for officers, communications equipment, computers		X
MO	Southeast Missouri Regional Crime Lab	Partial funding for renovation of a forensics laboratory that processes meth lab evidence, among others		X
MO	Wayne County Sheriff's Office	Computer supplies, vehicle insurance and supplies, training materials		X
MS	Jackson Co. Sheriff's Office	Safety equipment, training		X
MS	Mississippi Bureau of Narcotics	Vehicles, safety equipment and protective gear, chemical analysis equipment, training	X	
MS	Mississippi Bureau of Narcotics	Inter-agency coordination, collaborative community outreach, database maintenance		X
MT	Flathead County	Vehicles, surveillance and investigative equipment, chemical analysis and safety equipment, outreach, training		X
MT	Montana Division of Criminal Investigations	Research, personnel costs, vehicles, surveillance and safety equipment, forensic equipment and personnel, community outreach		X
ND	Minot State University Rural Crime and Justice Center	Community outreach, program development, technical assistance, program evaluation		X
NV	Nye County Sheriff's Department	Methamphetamine initiative	X	
NV	Sparks Police Department	Vehicle, surveillance equipment, training		X
OK	Bureau of Investigation	For costs associated with combating the production and distribution of methamphetamine.	X	
OK	City of Oklahoma	Personnel costs, contractor costs, equipment and supplies, outreach		X
OK	Oklahoma Bureau of Narcotics & Dangerous Drugs Control	Vehicles, responder equipment and supplies, training, safety equipment and supplies		X
OR	Marion County	Vehicles, surveillance and safety equipment, personnel costs. training		X
SD	Prairie View Prevention Services	Expand Community Mobilization Project to include prevention.	X	
SD	Prairie View Prevention Services	Training, personnel costs		X
UT	Iron County Sheriff's Office	Remote methamphetamine detection labs to identify damage caused by disposal of hazardous materials	X	

STATE	GRANTEE	RATIONALE	2001	2002
UT	Millard County Sheriff's Office	Personnel costs, training and safety equipment, evidence collection supplies, outreach		X
VA	Virginia Dept. of State Police	Surveillance equipment and supplies.	X	
VA	Virginia Dept. of State Police	Personnel costs, surveillance equipment, training, public outreach		X
VT	Vermont State Police Department	Multi-jurisdictional task force. Personnel costs, public outreach, training	X	X
WA	Washington Methamphetamine Initiative	Pierce County Alliance Information seminars, criminal justice training center, office equipment and supplies	X	
WA	Washington Methamphetamine Initiative	Pierce County Alliance Expansion of FY01 funded program		X
WI	Marathon Co. Sheriff's Office	Regional cooperation, equipment, training, outreach		X
WI	State Office of Justice	Presentation equipment, public outreach		X

Appendix B: Discretionary Grants, FY2001 and FY2002

STATE	GRANTEE	RATIONALE	YEAR	
			2001	2002
AL	Andalusia Police Department	SUV, surveillance and field communications equipment, computer equipment, training		X
AR	City of Pine Bluff	SUV, surveillance equipment, sampling and testing supplies, training materials		X
AR	Conway Police Department	Computer equipment and supplies, surveillance and communications equipment, GPS, training		X
AR	North Little Rock Police Dept.	AV equipment, safety equipment and personal protection supplies, training		X
AR	Searcy Police Department	GIS software and equipment, computers and related equipment, surveillance camera		X
AZ	Prescott Police Department	Laboratory equipment and supplies, personal protection supplies, trailer, tanks, portable waste pool, training		X
AZ	South Tucson Police Department	Laboratory equipment and supplies, personal protection supplies, trailer, tanks, portable waste pool, training		X
AZ	Pinal Co. Sheriff's Department	Utility van, generator, police radio, miscellaneous equipment		X
CA	Turlock Police Department	Computers and related equipment and supplies, AV equipment		X
CA	California Bureau of Narcotics	Training of state and local enforcement officers	X	
CA	California Department of Justice	Gas monitor, goggles, training courses		X
CA	Merced County	Funds provided upon review of request, if warranted.	X	
CO	Logan County Sheriff's Office	Vehicle, chemical monitors, laboratory and personal protection supplies, training		X
GA	Gainesville Police Department	Vehicle, generator, chemical testing kits, miscellaneous supplies		X
IA	Waterloo Police Department	Computer and equipment and supplies, surveillance and training equipment, software training		X
IL	Quincy Police Department	Search probe, communications equipment, camera, software		X
IN	Terre Haute Police Department	No description provided		X

KS	Cherokee Sheriff's Office	Trailer, communications and surveillance equipment, personal protection equipment	X
KS	Saline County Sheriff's Office	Surveillance and personal protection equipment	X
LA	Tangipahoa Sheriff's Office	Trailer, software, and surveillance, communications and personal protection equipment	X
LA	St. Tammany Parish Sheriff's Office	Chemical analysis and laboratory equipment and supplies, cameras, surveillance equipment, generator	X
MI	Allegan County Sheriff's Office	No description	X
MN	Blaine Police Department	Evidence supplies, testing kits, protective gear, training	X
MN	Minneapolis Police Department	Computers, safety equipment and supplies, surveillance equipment, presentation equipment	X
MO	Howell Co. Sheriff's Department	Computer	X
MS	Pearl River Sheriff's Office	Communications, surveillance, safety, and personal protection equipment, training	X
NM	Eddy County Sheriff's Dept.	Air sampling device	X
NV	Henderson Police Department	AV equipment, training	X
OR	Coos County Sheriff's Office	Training	X
OR	Douglas County Sheriff's Office	Surveillance equipment, training	X
SC	Lexington Police Department	Communications, surveillance, safety, and personal protection equipment and supplies, training	X
UT	Salt Lake City	Surveillance equipment, ion scanner, training, promotional and instructional materials	X

Appendix C: Conditions of Grant Award

1. Grantees which have been awarded funding for the procurement of an item in excess of $100,000 and plan to use a non-competitive procurement process must provide a written sole source justification to the COPS Office for approval prior to obligating, expending or drawing down grant funds for that item.

2. The funding under this project is for the payment of salaries, overtime, and approved benefits for sworn law enforcement officers and support personnel; equipment and technology; and training and/or travel that has been approved by the COPS Office. The allowable costs for which your grant has been approved are listed on the budget clearance memo, which is included in your award packet.

3. Methamphetamine Initiative grant funds must be used to supplement, and not supplant, local funds already committed for the grant purpose (hiring, purchases, and/or activities) that would exist in the absence of this grant. Grantees receiving Federal funds to pay for the salary and benefits of an employee must use the grant funds to hire a new, additional employee during the grant period. This newly hired employee may be dedicated to the Methamphetamine Initiative project or may be used to backfill a locally funded position if the locally funded individual is deployed to the Methamphetamine Initiative project.

4. Travel costs for transportation, lodging and subsistence, and related items are allowable under the Methamphetamine Initiative program with prior approval from the COPS Office. Payment for travel costs incurred directly by the grantee agency will be based on the rates established in the grantee's written travel policy, up to a maximum of the established federal rate for the relevant geographic area. Grantee agencies that do not have written travel policies will be funded at the established federal rate for the relevant geographic area. If grantee agencies are requesting Methamphetamine Initiative funds to pay for the grant related travel costs of other (non-grantee) individuals, those travel costs will be paid at the established federal rate for the relevant geographic area.

5. The grantee acknowledges its agreement to comply with the assurances and certifications submitted with the COPS Methamphetamine Initiative grant application.

6. The grantee acknowledges its agreement to comply with the Special Condition certification concerning potential environmental issues, which they have submitted to the COPS Office prior to the COPS Methamphetamine Initiative Grant Application. This certification mandates grantee compliance with Federal, State and local environmental, health and safety laws and regulations applicable to investigation, closure of clandestine methamphetamine laboratories and the removal and disposal of chemicals, equipment and wastes resulting from operations of these laboratories.

7. The recipients receiving funding under this grant program acquiesce that as the entity performing activities associated with the investigation and cleanup of clandestine methamphetamine laboratories that the recipient and not the COPS Office is the generator of hazardous chemical waste for the purposes of this project.

8. In order to assist the COPS Office in the monitoring of the award, your agency will be responsible for submitting annual program Status Update Reports (SUR) and quarterly Financial Status Reports (FSR).

9. The COPS Office may conduct or sponsor evaluations of the Methamphetamine Initiative program. The grantee agrees to cooperate with the evaluators to the extent practicable.

10. The grantee agrees to abide by the terms, conditions, and regulations as found in the Methamphetamine Initiative Grant Owner's Manual and the Uniform Administrative Requirements for Grants and Cooperative Agreements to State and Local Governments, 28 C.F.R. Part 66 (or the Uniform Administrative Requirements for Grants and Cooperative Agreements with Institutions of Higher Education, Hospitals and Other Non-profit Organizations, 28 C.F.R. Part 70 as applicable).

11. For grants of $500,000 or more (or $1,000,000 or more in grants over an 18-month period), the grantee acknowledges that failure to submit an acceptable Equal Employment Opportunity Plan (if grantee is required to submit one under 28 C.F.R. 42.302) that is approved by the Office of Justice Programs, Office of Civil Rights, is a violation of its Assurances and may result in the suspension of the drawdown of funds. For grants under $500,000 the grantee must submit a completed EEOP Certification form and return it to the Office of Justice Programs, Office of Civil Rights, within 60 days of the grant award.

12. You may request an extension of the grant award period to receive additional time to implement your grant program. These extensions do not provide additional funding. Only those grantees that can provide a reasonable justification for delays will be granted no-cost extensions.

13. The recipient agrees to complete and keep on file, as appropriate, an Immigration and Naturalization Service Employment Eligibility Verification Form (I-9). This form is to be used by the recipients of Federal funds to verify that persons are eligible to work in the United States.

14. The recipient will complete and submit to the El Paso Intelligence Center (EPIC) a form 143 for each clandestine methamphetamine laboratory that is seized and closed during the grant period.

15. Grantees using Methamphetamine Initiative funds to operate an interjurisdictional criminal intelligence system must comply with the operating principles of 28 C.F.R. Part 23. The grantee acknowledges that it has completed, signed, and submitted with its grant application the relevant special conditions certifying its compliance with 28 C.F.R. Part 23.

Appendix D:
Special Condition for Methamphetamine Initiative:
Mitigation of Health, Safety, and Environmental Risks

A.   <u>General Requirement</u>: The applicant agrees to comply with Federal, State, and local environmental, health, and safety laws and regulations applicable to the investigation and closure of clandestine methamphetamine laboratories and the removal and the disposal of the chemicals, equipment, and wastes used in or resulting from the operations of these laboratories.

B.   <u>Specific Requirements</u>: The applicant understands and agrees that any program or initiative involving either the identification, seizure, or closure of clandestine methamphetamine laboratories, hereafter referred to as the "Program," can result in adverse health, safety, and environmental impacts to (1) the law enforcement and other governmental personnel involved; (2) any residents, occupants, users, and neighbors of the site of a seized clandestine laboratory; (3) the seized laboratory site's immediate and surrounding environment; and (4) the immediate and surrounding environment of the site(s) where any remaining chemicals, equipment, and wastes from a seized laboratory's operations are placed or come to rest.

Therefore, the applicant further agrees that in order to avoid or mitigate the possible adverse health, safety, and environmental impacts of its Program, it will (1) include the nine, below listed protective measures or components within its Program; (2) provide for their adequate funding to include funding, as necessary, beyond that provided by the grant agreement; and (3) implement these protective measures throughout the life of the grant agreement. In so doing, the applicant understands that it may implement these protective measures directly through the use of its own resources and staff or may secure the qualified services of other agencies, contractors, or other qualified third parties.

The applicant agrees to include the following protective measures within its Program:

    1.   Provide medical screening of personnel assigned or to be assigned by the applicant to the seizure or closure of clandestine methamphetamine laboratories;

    2.   Provide Occupational Safety and Health Administration (OSHA) required initial and refresher training for law enforcement officials and other personnel assigned by the applicant to either the seizure or the closure of clandestine methamphetamine laboratories;

    3.   As determined by their specific duties, equip personnel assigned to the Program with OSHA required protective wear and other required safety equipment;

4.   Assign properly trained personnel to prepare a comprehensive contamination report on each closed laboratory;

5.   Employ qualified personnel to remove all chemicals and associated glassware, equipment, and contaminated materials and wastes from the site(s) of each seized clandestine laboratory;[65]

6.   Dispose of the chemicals, equipment, and contaminated materials and wastes removed from the sites of seized laboratories at properly licensed disposal facilities or, when allowable, properly licensed recycling facilities;

7.   Monitor the transport, disposal, and recycling components of subparagraphs numbered 5. and 6. immediately above in order to ensure proper compliance;

8.   Have in place and implement an inter-agency agreement or other form of commitment with a responsible state environmental agency that provides for that agency's (i) timely evaluation of the environmental conditions at and around the site of a closed clandestine laboratory and (ii) coordination with the responsible party, property owner, or others to ensure that any residual contamination is remediated, if necessary, and in accordance with existing state and federal requirements; and

9.   Include among the personnel involved in seizing clandestine methamphetamine laboratories, or have immediate access to, qualified personnel who can respond to the potential health needs of any of the offender(s)' children or other children present or living at the seized laboratory site. Response actions should include, at a minimum and as necessary, taking children into protective custody, immediately testing them for methamphetamine toxicity, and arranging for any necessary follow-up medical tests, examinations, or health care.

C.   Applicant's Acknowledgment and Agreement: Applicant acknowledges that it has received and reviewed the Environmental Assessment, including its appendices, and the Finding of No Significant Impact that have been prepared for this grant.

---

65 In order to be considered "qualified personnel," an individual must comply with all Federal, State, and local environmental, health and safety laws and regulations applicable to the removal of all chemicals and associated glassware, equipment, and contaminated materials and wastes from a clandestine laboratory, including but not limited to the applicable sections of: U.S. EPA's Resource Conservation and Recovery Act (RCRA), 40 C.F.R. Part 260, et seq., U.S. EPA's Comprehensive Environmental Response, Compensation and Liability Act (CERCLA), 40 C.F.R. Part 300, OSHA's Occupational Safety and Health Act, 29 C.F.R. Part 1910.120 and Part 1200, and U.S. Department of Transportation's regulations governing the labeling and transportation of hazardous materials and hazardous wastes, 49 C.F.R. Part 100, et seq. and Parts 350-399.

Applicant agrees to abide by the Environmental Assessment, including its appendices, and the Finding of No Significant Impact throughout the implementation of its Program. Applicant understands that this environmental assessment was prepared under the requirements of the National Environmental Policy Act, 42 U.S.C. 4321 et seq., and that this assessment provides both the basis for the above listed protective measures as well as references to several statutes, regulations, and guidelines that are particularly relevant to the implementation of these measures.

Certification

I certify that I have read the attached special condition and agree to abide by it:

_____

Signature of Law Enforcement Executive   Date

_____

Typed name of Law Enforcement Executive   Typed title of Law Enforcement
Executive

_____

Signature of Government Executive   Date

_____

Typed name of Government Executive   Typed title of Government Executive

Appendix E:

CERTIFICATION OF CLEANUP OF CLANDESTINE DRUG LABORATORIES

This section explains the requirements for cleanup of a clandestine drug laboratory discovered while implementing a Methamphetamine grant. It requires you to certify what cleanup strategy you plan on utilizing. Specifically, it requests certification regarding (1) the type of training local law enforcement personnel receive; (2) whether DEA contractors, DEA equivalent contractors or other qualified contractors and/or local personnel will perform the cleanup and disposal of hazardous chemical waste; and (3) whether vehicles and/or storage units funded under the grant program will be used to transport and/or store hazardous chemical waste. The acceptable cleanup strategies are discussed in more detail in the Environmental Assessment, which you reviewed and agreed to abide by prior to receiving these application materials.

In order to ensure protection of human health and the environment in implementing a COPS Methamphetamine grant, applicants must agree to the proper training of law enforcement personnel, the use of qualified contractors and/or local personnel for the clean up and disposal of hazardous waste, and the adherence to Federal, State and local regulatory requirements for the cleanup of hazardous chemical waste, including the transport and storage of such waste.

The training of law enforcement personnel must meet the requirements of the Occupational Safety and Health Administration (OSHA) regarding hazardous waste environments (29 CFR Part 1910.120 and part 1200) and the Environmental Protection Agency's (EPA) Resource Conservation and Recovery Act (RCRA) regulations pertaining to the generation, storage, transport, and disposal of hazardous wastes (40 CFR Parts 260 et seq.), as well as any State or local requirements.

In addition to ensuring the proper training of law enforcement personnel, the environmentally sound cleanup of clandestine laboratories is accomplished through the utilization of qualified contractors or local personnel who perform the duties of a "generator" of hazardous waste, as defined by the EPA in its regulations codified at 40 CFR Parts 260, *et seq.* 66 67

---

66 The Drug Enforcement Agency (DEA) undertakes cleanup of clandestine drug laboratories throughout the country by training agents under OSHA standards and by utilizing qualified contractors under the Hazardous Waste Cleanup and Disposal Contracts (HWCDC). Pending funding availability, DEA's services are available to all law enforcement agencies engaging in the cleanup of clandestine laboratories at no cost to the law enforcement agencies. As with the applicant's law enforcement personnel, the qualified contractor personnel must be trained under the requirements listed above and are responsible for utilizing permitted treatment, storage and disposal facilities that meet the above listed requirements

67 Although grantees under the COPS Methamphetamine grant must demonstrate how their clandestine drug laboratory cleanup program provides for the protection of human health and the environment, they are not required to either send their personnel specifically to the DEA training program or to use only DEA disposal contractors. However, if agencies choose not to use these existing DEA resources, they must demonstrate that they have equivalent training and disposal resources in place to include contractor oversight plans and procedures, or that the training and disposal resources in place meet applicable Federal, State and local laws and regulations.

An applicant's cleanup of hazardous chemical waste must also comply with EPA's Comprehensive Environmental Response Compensation and Liability Act (CERCLA) (40 CFR Part 300) and the US Department of Transportation's regulations governing the labeling and transportation of hazardous waste (Parts 49 CFR Part 100, et seq. and Parts 350-399).

Certifications

A. Clandestine Drug Laboratory Cleanup Program – Training of Law Enforcement Personnel

So that the COPS Office may ensure that your clandestine drug laboratory cleanup program adequately provides for the protection of human health and the environment in regard to the training of law enforcement personnel, please certify as to one of the following:

I certify that I will send my law enforcement personnel to the DEA training program pertaining to the cleanup of clandestine drug laboratories:

_____   _____
Signature of Law Enforcement Executive   Date

_____   _____
Typed name of Law Enforcement Executive   Typed title of Law Enforcement Executive

_____   _____
Signature of Government Executive   Date

_____   _____
Typed name of Government Executive   Typed title of Government Executive

I certify that I have DEA-equivalent ~~DEA equivalent~~ training in place for my law enforcement personnel regarding the cleanup of clandestine drug laboratories and that it meets the training requirements set forth in applicable Federal, State and local laws and regulations:

_____   _____
Signature of Law Enforcement Executive   Date

_____   _____
Typed name of Law Enforcement Executive   Typed title of Law Enforcement Executive

_____   _____
Signature of Government Executive   Date

_____   _____
Typed name of Government Executive   Typed title of Government Executive

I certify that I have training in place for my law enforcement personnel regarding the cleanup of clandestine drug laboratories and that it meets the training requirements set forth in applicable Federal, State and local laws and regulations:

_____   _____
Signature of Law Enforcement Executive   Date

_____   _____
Typed name of Law Enforcement Executive   Typed title of Law Enforcement Executive

_____   _____
Signature of Government Executive   Date

_____   _____
Typed name of Government Executive   Typed title of Government Executive

B.   Clandestine Drug Laboratory Cleanup Program – Disposal of Hazardous Waste

So that the COPS Office may ensure that your clandestine drug laboratory cleanup program adequately provides for the protection of human health and the environment in regard to the disposal of hazardous waste, please certify as to one of the following:

I certify that I will only utilize DEA disposal contractors for the cleanup and disposal of hazardous waste associated with clandestine drug laboratories:

_____   _____
Signature of Law Enforcement Executive   Date

_____   _____
Typed name of Law Enforcement Executive   Typed title of Law Enforcement Executive

_____   _____
Signature of Government Executive   Date

_____   _____
Typed name of Government Executive   Typed title of Government Executive

I certify that I will be using non-DEA disposal contractors for the cleanup and disposal of hazardous waste associated with clandestine drug laboratories, and that these contractors are DEA-equivalent and ~~are DEA-equivalent and~~ meet all necessary qualifications for the cleanup and disposal of hazardous waste*:

_____
Signature of Law Enforcement Executive

_____
Date

_____
Typed name of Law Enforcement Executive

_____
Typed title of Law Enforcement Executive

_____
Signature of Government Executive

_____
Date

_____
Typed name of Government Executive

_____
Typed title of Government Executive

I certify that I will be using non-DEA contractors and/or local government/law enforcement personnel for the cleanup and disposal of hazardous waste associated with clandestine drug laboratories, and that the individuals involved in these activities meet all necessary qualifications for the cleanup and disposal of hazardous waste*:

_____
Signature of Law Enforcement Executive

_____
Date

_____
Typed name of Law Enforcement Executive

_____
Typed title of Law Enforcement Executive

_____
Signature of Government Executive

_____
Date

_____
Typed name of Government Executive

_____
Typed title of Government Executive

C. Clandestine Drug Laboratory Cleanup Program – Funding for Vehicle and Storage Units

So that the COPS Office may ensure that the vehicles and storage containers that are funded under your clandestine drug laboratory cleanup program adequately provides for the protection of human health and the environment in regard to the transport and storage of hazardous chemical waste, please certify as to one of the following:

I certify that funding received under this program for vehicles and/or storage units for the specific purpose of transporting and/or storing chemical hazardous waste meets the requirements set forth in applicable Federal, State and local laws and regulations.

_____   _____
Signature of Law Enforcement Executive   Date

_____   _____
Typed name of Law Enforcement Executive   Typed title of Law Enforcement Executive

_____   _____
Signature of Government Executive   Date

_____   _____
Typed name of Government Executive   Typed title of Government Executive

I certify that funding received for vehicles and/or storage units under this project were not awarded for the specific purpose of transporting and/or storing chemical hazardous waste and will not be used for such activities associated with the cleanup of clandestine laboratories.

_____   _____
Signature of Law Enforcement Executive   Date

_____   _____
Typed name of Law Enforcement Executive   Typed title of Law Enforcement Executive

_____   _____
Signature of Government Executive   Date

_____   _____
Typed name of Government Executive   Typed title of Government Executive

Appendix F:
FY 2002 Methamphetamine Initiative
List of Allowable Costs

The following information summarizes categories of allowable and unallowable costs for funding from COPS under the Methamphetamine Initiative. The budget items must programmatically link to the activities described in the proposal. While costs may be listed as allowable, the COPS Office will determine appropriateness of requested funds for the activities within each proposal. The burden to adequately demonstrate that the item requested is directly related to the program is placed on the grantee and the COPS Office may delete any unlinked items without notification.

Although some of the statutory application requirements for COPS grants have been waived for the COPS Methamphetamine Initiative, the prohibition against supplanting remains in force. That is, funds provided must be in addition to locally budgeted items, not in lieu of these items.

Personnel

Law Enforcement officers
- Approved overtime incurred after the award start date for existing full-time officers working directly on this program

Employees other than law enforcement officers (civilian support staff)
- Salaries and benefits of support staff hired after your award start date to work directly on this program;
- Salaries and benefits of support staff hired after your award start date to backfill a vacancy created when your agency re-deploys an experienced locally funded civilian to the COPS grant project.

NOTE: When itemizing fringe benefits, FICA combined with Social Security cannot exceed 7.65 percent, and if you are not requesting reimbursement for FICA, Worker's Compensation or Unemployment, please make a note that your agency plans to cover these items, or provide an explanation for why your agency does not pay them.

Travel

- Reasonable out of town travel costs (lodging, meals, and transportation costs if travel is over 50 miles from program location) in accordance with applicable guidelines to visit other jurisdictions engaged in similar programs or to attend conferences/training directly related to the goals of the program.

Technology and Equipment

NOTE: Any expenses under $5,000 per unit should be itemized under "Supplies."

- Technology and equipment that is purchased specifically for this program after the award start date and can be clearly linked to the implementation or enhancement of the program. The burden is on the grantee to adequately demonstrate this connection. (Some potential examples may include computerized crime analysis software, mapping software, or electronic bulletin boards to enhance communication between police and citizens.)

Supplies

- Supplies such as copying, general office items, postage and others if directly related to the program.

Consultants/Contracts

- Consultant/contractor costs if they directly contribute to the implementation or enhancement of the program (Note: Consulting may not exceed $450 per day without prior approval by the COPS Office.);
- Consultant or trainer fees only for additional training that supplements, but does not replace, any current training of new or re-deployed officers, civilians, and/or community members in areas or topics that relate to the programs goals;
- Supervisory training related to the program; and
- Conference costs related to the program (registration fees, books).

Other Costs

- Performance evaluation development;
- Publications relating to the program and community policing;
- Reasonable and appropriate community incentives (subcontracts, awards, etc.);
- Local evaluation costs;
- Examples of these costs include: small contracts with local colleges and universities, in-house research staff costs, and focused technology costs;
- Training development costs directly related to the program;
- Costs related to survey development, administration, and analysis of survey information;
- In-house newsletters;
- Partnership or team building costs including travel, focus group meetings, and other related activities (note, however, that meals and refreshments for meetings are not allowed);
- Video production if directly related to the program;
- Costs of community meetings and workshops, including reasonable room rental costs; and
- Internet access fees, on-line research services, etc. if directly related to the program.

Appendix G:
FY 2002 Methamphetamine Initiative
List of Unallowable Costs

**Items will be reviewed on a case-by-case basis, however, agencies are expected to request items that are linked to the parameters stipulated in the DOJ Appropriation Act, 2002, Public Law 107-77. In addition, departments must demonstrate that these items have a direct correlation to their overall Methamphetamine project objectives and that without said items the project could not be implemented. The COPS Office will review an applicant's request based on the feasibility and totality of the circumstances surrounding the jurisdiction's methamphetamine problem. Historically, the item categories that have consistently not been funded are indirect costs, response-oriented equipment, items that are funded through the local department budget, and general office supplies.

Personnel:
- Salaries and benefits of existing officers.
- Salaries and benefits of existing employees.
- Salaries and benefits of grant writers or other staff that do not directly contribute to the implementation of the program.
- Overtime: For personnel not directly involved in the department's project and that which exceeds 20% of total budget.
- Fringe benefits for overtime of existing employees.

Travel:
- Local travel costs (lodging, meals, *per diem*, transportation costs, mileage reimbursement) within a 50-mile radius of the location.
- Parking fees, taxi fare.
- Meals and/or refreshment costs associated with meetings.

Response-Oriented Technology and Equipment:
- Bunker shield(s)
- Standard issue uniforms
- Animals
- Bulletproof vests and accessories
- Bicycles
- Radar guns
- Dictation systems
- Television / VCR(s)
- Phone lines and voice-mail systems (hotlines will be considered)
- Handcuffs, weapons, and ammunition
- Standard office furniture and equipment
- Office rental space, lease (*copiers, fax machines, desks, chairs, shredders, etc.*)
- Cellular phones
- Construction and Renovation costs
- PDAs and pagers (including service time)
- Police vehicles (*patrol cars, mobile police units, surveillance and leased vehicles*).
- Standard issue police vehicle equipment (*including light bars, cages, and siren packages*)
- Equipment for surveillance vehicles used specifically in the DEC project will be

considered.

Supplies:
- Standard office supplies not directly related to the Methamphetamine Initiative.
- Indirect costs.

Consultants and Contracts:
- Training in topics that are not directly linked to the Methamphetamine Initiative (DEC).
- Contractual agreements which cannot be directly linked to the Methamphetamine Initiative.
- Maintenance and/or service contracts that extend the life of the initial grant period; (multi-year contracts are allowable, but must be paid in full up-front within the one-year life of the grant).
- Any consultant fees in excess of $450 per day need to receive prior approval from the COPS Office, contingent upon written justification by the grantee.

Clean-up Costs:
Costs associated with the clean-up of clandestine drug laboratories utilizing contractors who are not qualified to dispose of hazardous waste and/or where the applicant does not have DEA-equivalent disposal resources in place to include contractor oversight plans and procedures.

Note: Please refer to the Environmental Assessment that was provided to your agency prior to receiving your proposal kit for further explanation of qualified contractors.

Appendix H:
Types of Activities and Associated Equipment Requests

For each activity, the equipment list is provided only as examples, not as a comprehensive list of all equipment requested by grantees.

Types	Activities	Equipment	
Outreach and Office Operations			
Methamphetamine Database management	Database used to track arrest data, seizure date, presence of children, precursors, agent workload, lab type, purity of drug, demographics	▪ Laptops ▪ Computer upgrade ▪ Multi media computer	▪ Color printer ▪ Software
General Office Activities	Presentations	▪ Interactive video conferencing connection ▪ Projectors (video, presentations)	▪ Digital tape recorder w/ pen microphones ▪ Laser pointer
Outreach	Informing the public about dangers of methamphetamine and recognizing clandestine laboratories	▪ DEC Conference ▪ Paper office supplies ▪ Information booklets	▪ Displays/banners ▪ Projector ▪ Surveys
Training			
Clandestine lab entry certification training	Recertification of agents	▪ Safety equipment (see Removal Action) ▪ NES Field Guidebook ▪ NIOSH Field Guidebook	
Other training	Drug Recognition training First response investigative Training for school outreach program Covert surveillance training Undercover narcotics training Meth Enforcement training Education-Intervention Program Drug Symptomology Hazardous Waste Operations training The COPS Methamphetamine Conference	▪ Working meals (per diem) ▪ Laptop computer ▪ Training materials ▪ Students' cost to attend school ▪ Classroom rental ▪ Travel expenses ▪ Printed material ▪ Safety equipment (see Removal Action)	
Chemical analysis training	Investigation and identification of drugs, drug residue and components used to cut drugs	▪ High wattage lasers ▪ Ion scanners	
Law Enforcement Activities			
Drug diversion investigations	Precursor theft and investigation of methamphetamine distribution	▪ Anhydrous ammonia nurse tank locks	
Surveillance of potential clandestine laboratory	Monitoring of suspects and laboratory	▪ Infrared light ▪ Bodywire ▪ Portable X-ray ▪ Color pinhole camera	▪ Low light black/white camera ▪ Zoom binoculars ▪ Ground sensor ▪ High wattage lasers

Field communications	Assist communication and coordination of agents during surveillance and single- and multi-site raids	• Digital transmitter/recorder • Digital receiver • Portable radio with charger units • Radio encryption and modification systems • Handheld GPS	• Microwave video receiver • Digital cell phone • AC wall outlet audio transmitter • Radio microphone/head sets • Mobile radio repeater system
Seizure of suspects	Protection of law enforcement officers during entry into laboratory	• Tactical jumpsuits • Gas masks • Protective suits • Protective boots • Waterproof boots	• Portable eye wash system • Airpack for assisted breathing • Air monitoring equipment
Seizure of laboratory equipment	Sampling of chemicals and drugs found in laboratory	• Respirators • Pipettes and tubes • Vials • Auto Vial insert • Sample bottles • Teflon caps • pH strips • Drop cloths • Tubs	• Evidence testing kits • Supply cases • Sampling supplies • Camper shells • Latent print lift kits • Canister adapter • MPC canister • Rehab fan • Snap fold modular tent
Sampling of crime scene	Sampling of evidence	• Sampling kit • Smoke/fog machine • Pipettes • Glass vials • Fire-proof evidence safe	• Nitrile bottles • pH strips • Cameras/camcorders • Evidence testing kits
Removal Actions			
Safety Equipment	Protection of agents during entry into clandestine laboratory and exposure to chemicals or hazardous waste	• Tactical jumpsuits • Gas masks • Protective suits • Protective boots • Waterproof boots • Safety glasses • Gloves • Medical kits • SCBA with mask & harness	• SCBA voice amplifier • Airpack for SCBA • Carbon cylinder for airpack • Portable eye wash system • PAN disruptor assembly (bomb equipment) • Explosion-proof flashlights
Hazardous waste removal	Transport of hazardous waste from clandestine laboratory	• Pickup trucks, response vehicles	
	Hazardous waste removal action	• Plastic sheets • Buckets • Containers	• Duct tape • Decontamination solvents • Rope
Transportation			
Vehicles	Transport personnel to and from clandestine laboratory location including agents, investigators, tactical teams, and support personnel	• Command post vehicle • SUVs for Narcotics K9 Team • Personnel decontamination showers and eye wash station • Lab response vehicle • Rehab/support trailer	

	Transport equipment such as radios, field meters, toxic gas detectors, cameras, respirators and optical equipment, safety equipment	• 4WD, all-terrain vehicle • Extended cab pickup • Cargo trailer	• Pickup trucks • Safety processing vehicles
	Transport hazardous waste from clandestine laboratory location to storage unit and, in certain cases, to the disposal site.	• Waste disposal vehicle • Painting and identification markers	
Disposal			
Disposal fees	Hazardous waste disposal or recycling costs	• Pay fees to disposal facility	
Other Activities			
Chemical Analysis	In-house analysis of chemical found at clandestine methamphetamine laboratories	• Gas chromatograph-mass spectrometer system • Ionization Scanners • Lasers with accessories • Accessory module	• Gas tech air monitoring • Drug screening system • Imagers (e.g. digital thermal imager) • Scanning electron microscope
Laboratory analysis		• Funding for laboratory technicians • Lab renovation and expansion	
Drug Endangered Children Program		• Ion scanners • Medical monitoring	
Personnel	New personnel hired with grant funding include administrative assistants, intelligence analysts, dedicated prosecutors, and agents and troopers	• Physical health examinations for officers • Salaries for new personnel • Benefits • Overtime	
Miscellaneous		• Office security cameras • Security monitoring service • Portable generator • Audio/alarm cellular transmitter	• Fold-up hoist • Photo quality paper • Batteries • Camera film • Mylar film

Appendix I:
Selected State Initiative Descriptions

The DOJ COPS Office Methamphetamine Initiative provided discretionary and earmarked grant funding for methamphetamine initiatives in several dozen states in 2001 and 2002. These descriptions focus on typical grant funded activities for state and local methamphetamine initiatives as well as unique aspects of initiatives in California, Hawaii, Missouri, Washington, Iowa, Wisconsin, and Arkansas. Detailed lists of grant-funded initiatives are included in Appendices A and B.

California

Grant funds have been provided to several California methamphetamine initiatives including the California Methamphetamine Strategy Program (CALMS). Grant funding is not generally used to fund hazardous waste removal actions in California. The State Department of Toxic Substances conducts, and pays for out of general state revenues, approximately 95 percent of the clandestine drug laboratory hazardous waste removal actions. The Department conducted removal actions at 2208 clandestine drug laboratory sites in 2002. However, as there is no requirement that state or local law enforcement authorities use the Department's services some state and local authorities may be conducting their own removal actions, storage and disposal. At present, no grant funding has been applied to conduct of hazardous waste removal actions in California. State and local authorities conducting such removal actions (whether or not such activities are grant funded) are responsible for complying with RCRA regulations, DOT regulations, California hazardous waste manifest requirements, and the California Environmental Quality Act (CEQA) requirements. According to the CEQA Coordinator for the California Methamphetamine Initiative, clandestine drug laboratory law enforcement actions and associated hazardous waste removal actions are exempt from CEQA because they are "emergency" actions.

California regulations require all hazardous waste generators, regardless of generator status, to manifest waste shipments. The State Department of Toxic Substances program for transporting, storing and disposing of waste is itself subject to CEQA. Storage of hazardous waste at a transfer location for more than ten days, or any treatment or repackaging of the waste at a transfer location, would require a state hazardous waste storage facility permit and would trigger CEQA. The State avoids CEQA by requiring, by contract, their emergency response contractors to store waste for less than the 10-day limit before transporting the waste to a permitted TSDF. The State Department of Toxic Substances inspects the emergency response contractor facilities biannually to ensure that regulatory and contract requirements are being met. State hazardous waste management contractors are required to implement security requirements (fencing) so that material cannot be diverted. Hazardous waste is stored outdoors in the emergency response contractor's equipment yards (the same place that the contractor's emergency response vehicles and equipment are stored.) There are seven state-contracted emergency response contractors that service different parts of the state. Response time for hazardous waste removal actions for clandestine drug laboratory seizures is on the order of two hours.

Hawaii

Grant funds have been provided to the Narcotics Enforcement Division of the State of Hawaii.[68] The funds enable the payment of overtime hours and benefits for sworn and non-sworn law enforcement officers and civilian personnel, including inspectors, analysts, and computer programmers, and the purchase of equipment. Grant funding has been used to fund training and medical clearance exams for law enforcement Personnel on the Clandestine Laboratory Investigations Support Team (CLIST). This training is required by OSHA regulations for personnel to use APR and SCBA.

Grant funding has also been used to pay hazardous waste contractors to conduct hazardous waste removal actions and associated transportation, storage, and disposal costs. The State of Hawaii initiative has

---

[68] FY2002 COPS Methamphetamine Initiative, Hawaii Methamphetamine Program Budget Narrative

employed the same hazardous waste management contractor as DEA employs in Hawaii to conduct hazardous waste removal actions, transportation, storage, and disposal. The contractor has been employed during multi-agency responses to clandestine drug laboratories throughout the State of Hawaii. Funding for removal actions has been provided in part by the grant program, and in part through the DEA National Clandestine Laboratory Cleanup Program.

Missouri

Missouri grant funded initiatives have used grant funds for payment of overtime salaries, purchases of operating supplies, vehicles, equipment and supplies and to fund hazardous waste disposal fees and administration fees.[69] The MSSC Regional Crime Lab utilized grant funding to purchase two modern gas chromatographs and a mass spectrometer system for processing of evidence and environmental samples in a chemical analytical laboratory. The City of Boonville grant funds have been used to provide overt and covert narcotics assistance to law enforcement agencies. In partnership with MUSTANG (Mid-Missouri Unified Strike Team and Narcotics Group), the City of Boonville also developed a program to actively pursue persons procuring and/or stealing the needed precursors for the manufacture of methamphetamine.

There are approximately 12 hazardous waste "bunker units" located through Missouri for use by state and local law enforcement agencies for temporary storage of hazardous waste. All but one of these units are located at fire stations and are "manned" by Hazmat-trained firefighters. The Missouri Department of Natural Resources (DNR) acquired the "bunker units" approximately three years ago in order to improve response time. DEA contractors were based in Kansas City, Missouri, and in Tulsa, Oklahoma. During the transit time from their bases to the remote locations of clandestine drug laboratories in Missouri, state/local law enforcement personnel had to work overtime for 5 hours or more to secure the laboratory. Siting hazardous waste "bunker units" throughout the state and training law enforcement officers to package and transport waste was done to improve response time. Funding from the DOJ COPS Office Methamphetamine Initiative has been applied to the operation of these "bunker units."

The Missouri DNR provides a six to eight hour course to law enforcement officers to "bunker certify" them to use these "bunker units." Law enforcement officers who are not trained by Missouri DNR are not authorized to use the "bunker units." The law enforcement officers do not have to be "lab certified" to use the "bunker units." Missouri DNR also provides "lab certification" training to law enforcement personnel, and Missouri DNR and the Missouri highway patrol provide "lab re-certification program" training to law enforcement personnel. For the approximately 11 "manned" units, the law enforcement officer calls ahead to the fire station and is met by a Hazmat trained fireman, who transfers the hazardous waste to the "bunker unit." For the "unmanned" unit, the law enforcement officer picks up a key for the unit (and for the surrounding security fence and gate) and transfers the hazardous waste into the unit him/herself.

Officers transporting hazardous wastes are required to segregate containers (flammables, oxidizers, corrosives) into separate shelves of the storage unit. The storage units are equipped with shelves and dividers to facilitate waste segregation. There is a "log sheet" that the officer fills out indicating that the unit has been used and what hazardous wastes were placed in the unit. The officer also fills out the "EPIC" data form that indicates what hazardous wastes were recovered from the laboratory site. The bunker unit locations are equipped with "lab trash barrels" that are used to manage contaminated personal protective equipment (gloves), "empty" containers, etc. generated through hazardous waste management activities.

Washington

Grant funds have been to the Washington Methamphetamine Initiative, and allocated by the state to several agencies, and approximately 52 jurisdictions.[70] Enforcement funding has been used for the hiring and

---

[69] COPS Methamphetamine Initiative, Report to House and Senate Appropriations Committees, Methamphetamine Grants Awarded in FY 2002.
[70] FY2002 COPS Methamphetamine Initiative, Washington State Methamphetamine Initiative Project Summary

equipping of detectives in 24 counties to handle precursor chemical investigations. One Washington grantee, under the funds allocated for treatment/family services developed a model treatment program that deals with dependency issues of abusive parents or parents addicted to methamphetamine. Grants have been allocated to Washington State Division of Alcohol and Substance Abuse to expand this treatment program to two other counties in Western and Eastern Washington. Public education programs that increased public awareness and mobilized local communities to deal with methamphetamine problems were activated in 28 new counties using grant funding.

The Washington Department of Health and Department of Ecology (WDOH and WDOE) have been allocated grant funds to sustain the overtime needed to conduct removal actions and fund the associated hazardous waste transportation and storage activities and hazardous waste disposal fees. Hazardous waste disposal is conducted at county-operated "moderate risk waste" disposal facilities and also at commercial hazardous waste disposal facilities.[71] Grant funds have also been used by the WDOE to purchase a laboratory response vehicle that is equipped with a covered, isolated cargo space for transporting hazardous waste and equipped with outside lockers for transport of tools and supplies. Funds allocated to the Lewis County Sheriff's Department for law enforcement have been expended to provide for the temporary storage of hazardous (or potentially hazardous) materials recovered by sheriff's deputies in a certified storage facility until WDOE can remove the materials[72].

Iowa

Grant funding has been provided to three Iowa methamphetamine initiatives.[73] Funding awarded to the Iowa Regional Methamphetamine Training Center supported the Tri-State Regional Methamphetamine Training Center that targets small rural agencies. Training is focused on Clandestine Lab Enforcement, Undercover Operations, Warrant Preparation and Service, Tactical Warrant Service, Highway Interdiction, Police Officer Safety, and Safety Issues for Fire/Rescue personnel. The Governors Office of Drug Control Policy carried out a program on reducing the availability of anhydrous ammonia by utilizing the entire award to purchase anhydrous ammonia nurse tank locks. Nurse tanks are used in agriculture to supply anhydrous ammonia to agricultural fields. The nurse tank lock program is intended to prevent theft of anhydrous ammonia from the tanks and diversion of the ammonia to methamphetamine production.

Wisconsin

Grant funding has been provided to several Wisconsin Methamphetamine Initiative programs.[74] The largest portion of the grant funds awarded to the Wisconsin Division of Narcotic Enforcement (DNE) was used to purchase specialized chemical analytical equipment. GPS trackers are used for live or historical tracking of suspect vehicles. Drager Accuro pumps are used for taking air samples at clandestine drug laboratory sites to test for hydrochloric acid, nitric acid and ammonia. Grant funds have also been used to purchase and equip two clandestine drug laboratory response trailers. These trailers are used to transport safety equipment, chemical decontamination supplies, and surveillance equipment to clandestine drug laboratory sites. Additional grant funds have been used for Clan Lab Certification training of law enforcement

---

[71] "Moderate-risk waste" (MRW) is defined in the Washington Hazardous Waste Management Act as household waste and CESQG waste. Washington County Governments operate a system of MRW collection facilities throughout the state. These facilities are used to manage hazardous waste generated from clandestine drug laboratory removal actions. In some areas of the state where MRW collection facilities are not available, it is necessary to use commercial disposal facilities for disposal of hazardous wastes.

[72] In Lewis County the local law enforcement jurisdiction owns and operates the hazardous waste storage unit, and WDOE, periodically, using grant-funded "disposal fees", picks up the hazardous waste from the storage unit and transports it to disposal sites. WDOE or local law enforcement agencies may transport the hazardous waste from the removal action location to the storage location.

[73] Report to House and Senate Appropriations Committees, Methamphetamine Grants Awarded in FY 2002.

[74] FY2002 COPS Methamphetamine Initiative, Wisconsin Methamphetamine Initiative Project Summary and Budget Narrative

---

officers, and for public awareness enhancement.

Arkansas

The Arkansas State Police recently filed an amendment to its grant application, seeking to reprogram certain funds.[75] The Arkansas Initiative requested funding to equipment to determine whether children residing at clandestine drug laboratory locations have been exposed to controlled substances to promote enforcement of a recently proposed child endangerment statute. The Arkansas Initiative has also requested funding to purchase air purifying respirators (APRs) for use by "non-certified" investigators who are first responders and who may assist certified investigators after the clandestine drug laboratory scene has been evaluated, but while APRs are still required to enter the scene. Although personnel using the APRs for the purposes of law enforcement would need to be trained in their use, the Arkansas Initiative has not requested grant funding to provide such training in their grant revision application.

The Arkansas Initiative has also requested grant funding to establish a centralized pickup site located at the Arkansas State Crime Laboratory for chemical analytical laboratory wastes generated by laboratory chemists working at clandestine drug laboratory sites. The laboratory chemists would package the hazardous wastes and transport the hazardous wastes to the central pickup site as part of their normal job activities, and DEA contractors would fund the transportation of the hazardous waste from the pickup site to a disposal site. Therefore grant funding would be applied only to establishing the pickup site, not for construction activities.

Other Grant Funded Initiatives

The Phoenix Arizona Police Department has used grant funding to administer Clandestine Laboratory Site Safety training to certify law enforcement personnel as OSHA Site Safety Officers, and for law enforcement officers to attend HAZMAT training administered by the Phoenix Fire Department. The Phoenix Police Department continues to use DEA contractors to conduct (non grant-funded) hazardous waste removal actions, such as conduct of removal actions that fall outside the purview of the DEA.[76]

The Indiana State Police Department and Terre Haute Police Department have applied grant funding to conduct hazardous waste removal actions and to pay hazardous waste disposal fees. The Indiana Department uses forensic scientists to manage small amounts of hazardous waste and disposes of the hazardous waste using a contract service, and uses DEA contractors to manage hazardous wastes recovered from larger laboratories. Indiana has also applied grant funding to purchase safety processing vehicles and safety trailers that are used to transport personal protective equipment and other safety equipment to clandestine drug laboratory sites. A separate grant-funded waste disposal vehicle is used to transport hazardous waste recovered from clandestine drug laboratory sites.[77] Kansas applied grant funding to purchase safety equipment trailers, communications and surveillance equipment, personal protective equipment, chemical analytical laboratory supplies, and vehicles (including a hazmat response vehicle), and training in the use of personal protective equipment. Utah applied grant funding to support remote methamphetamine detection laboratories to identify damage caused by disposal of hazardous materials, and purchase all-terrain vehicles and trailers to enable access to remote, off road clandestine drug laboratory locations.

---

[75] FY2003 Grant Revision – Arkansas State Police Coordinated Methamphetamine Initiative, January 2003.
[76] FY2002 COPS Methamphetamine Initiative, Phoenix Police Department Methamphetamine Laboratory Cleanup Grant Application, Project Summary.
[77] FY2002 COPS Methamphetamine Initiative, Indiana Methamphetamine Initiative II Expanded Budget Detail Information.

Appendix J:
Health Hazards of Chemicals Used in Methamphetamine Production

Chemical Name	Health Effects	Chemical Incompatibilities
2,5Dimethoxybenzaldehyde	N/A	N/A
Acetic Anhydride	Highly corrosive liquid that can irritate nose, throat, mouth, eyes, and skin. Exposure to high doses can result in permanent eye damage and lung damage with coughing and/or shortness of breath.	Strong oxidizing agents, strong reducing agents, bases, alcohols, metal powders, moisture.
Acetone/ Ethyl Alcohol	Extremely flammable, posing a fire risk in and around the laboratory. Inhalation or ingestion of these solvents causes severe gastric irritation, narcosis, or coma.	Strong oxidizing agents, strong acids, perchlorates, aliphatic amines, chromyl chloride, hexachloromelamine, chromic anhydride, chloroform + alkali, potassium tert-butoxide.
Anhydrous Ammonia	A colorless gas with a pungent, suffocating odor. Inhalation causes edema of the respiratory tract and asphyxia. Contact with vapors damages eyes and mucous membranes.	Mercury (e.g. in pressure gauges), chlorine, calcium hypochlorite, iodine, bromine, and hydrogen fluoride
Anthranilic Acid	Yellowish crystal. Dust can irritate skin, eyes, and respiratory tract. Harmful if swallowed.	Strong oxidizing agents.
Butylamine	Flammable liquid and fire hazard. Vapors can irritate nose, throat, eyes, and skin. Higher exposures can cause pulmonary edema (build-up of fluid in lungs).	Oxidizing agents.
Cyclohexanone	Inhalation can irritate eyes, nose, and throat causing coughing and wheezing. Exposure to high doses can cause dizziness, and passing out, and cataracts.	Oxidizing agents and nitric acid.
Ephedrine	Skin, eye and respiratory irritant. Chronic use can lead to hypersensitization. High doses can cause headaches, dizziness, trembling, sweating, irregular heartbeat, nervousness, and paleness.	Strong acids, acid chlorides, acid anhydrides, and strong oxidizing agents.
Ergometrine	Can cause gangrene, headache, abdominal pain, and allergic phenomena (including shock, hypertension, chest pain, and palpitation.	N/A
Ethyl Acetate	Flammable liquid and fire hazard. Inhalation irritates nose, throat, skin, and eyes. Exposure to high levels causes dizziness and passing out.	Strong acids, strong oxidizers, and strong bases.
Ethyl Ether	Highly flammable liquid and dangerous fire hazard. When breathed, can cause drowsiness, excitement, irregular breathing, unconsciousness, and death. High exposure can affect kidneys.	Peroxides, combustible materials, halogens, oxidizing materials, metal salts, acids, bases.
Ethylamine	Highly flammable liquid and dangerous fire hazard. Can irritate eyes, nose, throat, and lungs when inhaled. Repeated exposure may damage liver, kidneys, and heart.	Strong acids (such as hydrochloric, sulfuric, and nitric) and strong oxidizers (such as chlorine, bromine, and fluorine).

Chemical Name	Health Effects	Chemical Incompatibilities
Formamide	When breathed, can irritate nose and throat and damage male reproductive glands. Contact can cause eye irritation, burns, and skin rash.	Iodine, pyridine, and sulfur trioxide.
Formic Acid	A corrosive acid that can irritate skin, eyes, and respiratory system, with possible permanent eye damage. May cause mutations, nausea, headache, and dizziness. Ingestion or inhalation may result in kidney or liver damage.	Oxidizing agents (such as permanganates and nitrates), strong acids (such as hydrochloric, sulfuric, and nitric), strong bases (such as sodium hydroxide), and finely powdered metals.
Hydriodic Acid	A corrosive acid with vapors that are irritating to the respiratory system, eyes, and skin. If ingested, causes severe internal irritation and damage that may cause death.	Metals, oxidizing materials, peroxides, halogens, and combustible materials.
Hydrochloric Acid	Colorless gas or fuming liquid can cause burns to respiratory tract, skin, eyes, and mucous membranes. May also cause frostbite, blindness, and liver and kidney damage.	Strong bases, amines, oxidizing agents, organic materials, metal carbides, and sulfuric acid. Reacts with metals to form hydrogen gas, which is highly flammable and explosive.
Iodine and Iodine Crystals	Gives off vapor that is irritating to respiratory system and eyes. Solid form irritates the eyes and may burn skin. If ingested, it will cause severe internal damage.	Acetylene, ammonia (laboratory gas of solution)
Lithium Metal	Extremely caustic to all body tissues. Reacts violently with water and poses a fire or explosion hazard.	Moisture, acids, oxidizers, oxygen, nitrogen, carbon dioxide, temperatures above melting point (180.5 °C/357 °F).
Methamphetamine Liquid		
Methyl Ethyl Ketone	Inhalation can cause headaches, nausea, and irritation of the eyes and respiratory tract; high doses can also result in narcosis. Eye contact with liquid form can cause corneal injury.	Caustics (such as sodium hydroxide), amines, alkanolamines, aldehydes, ammonia, strong oxidizing agents, and chlorinating compounds.
Methylamine	Highly flammable colorless gas or liquid causing severe irritation of eyes, skin, and respiratory tract when inhaled. Repeated exposure may cause bronchitis.	Mercury, copper, zinc, aluminum and galvanized surfaces, flammable materials, and strong oxidizers (such as chlorine, chlorine dioxide, and bromine).
n-Acetylanthranilic Acid	Harmful if swallowed. Eye, skin, and respiratory irritant.	Strong oxidizing agents.
n-Ethylephedrine	N/A	N/A
Nitroethane	Flammable liquid. May be harmful if swallowed, inhaled, or absorbed through skin. Causes eye irritation. Absorption into body leads to methemoglobinemia resulting in cyanosis (blue lips).	Oxidizing agents, amines, acids, alkalis, hydrocarbon mixtures, metal oxides.
o-Toluidine	Combustible liquid and vapor. Suspected cancer hazard. May be fatal if swallowed, inhaled, or absorbed through skin. Causes irritation to skin, eyes, and respiratory tract. Affects blood, kidneys, liver, and cardiovascular system.	Oxidizing agents, strong acids, and strong bases.

Chemical Name	Health Effects	Chemical Incompatibilities
Phenethylamine	Combustible liquid and vapor. Contact with skin has a defatting effect, causing drying and irritation. Liquid may cause permanent eye damage.	Strong oxidizing agents, strong acids.
Phenyl-2-propanone (P2P)	Can be harmful if swallowed, inhaled, or absorbed through skin. Causes irritation to skin, eyes, and respiratory tract.	Strong oxidizing and reducing agents, strong bases.
Phenylacetic Acid	A corrosive acid that may cause respiratory and digestive tract irritation. Causes eye and skin burns. May cause reproductive and fetal effects.	Strong oxidizing agents, strong bases.
Potassium Permanganate	Strong oxidizer that may cause fire when in contact with other materials. Causes irritation to skin, eyes, and respiratory tract. Ingestion of solid or high concentrations causes severe distress of gastro-intestinal system and may be fatal.	Powdered metals, alcohol, arsenites, bromides, iodides, phosphorous, sulfuric acid, organic compounds, sulfur, activated carbon, hydrides, strong hydrogen peroxide, ferrous or mercurous salts, hypophosphites, hyposulfites, sulfites, peroxides, and oxalates.
Pseudoephedrine	Ingestion of doses greater than 240 mg. causes hypertension, arrhythmia, anxiety, dizziness, and vomiting. Ingestion of doses greater than 600 mg. can lead to renal failure and seizures.	Strong oxidizing agents.
Red Phosphorus	May explode on contact or friction. Ignites if heated above 260oF. Vapor from ignited phosphorus severely irritates the nose, throat, lungs, and eyes.	Halogens, halides, sulfur, and oxidizing materials (may explode on contact).
Safrole	Carcinogen and mutagen. Contact may irritate skin. High exposure can cause nausea, vomiting, headache, dizziness, drowsiness, convulsions or unconsciousness. May cause liver damage.	Oxidizing agents.
Sodium Dichromate	Carcinogen and potentially fatal if swallowed. Inhalation, ingestion, and skin absorption are harmful to skin, eyes, and respiratory tract.	Strong reducing agents, strong acids, organic materials, and combustible materials.
Sodium Metal	May cause burns to skin, eyes, and respiratory tract. Reacts violently with water; extremely corrosive in the presence of moisture.	Oxidizing and reducing agents, acids, combustible materials, halo carbons, halogens, amines, metals, metal oxides, metal salts, bases.
Sulfuric Acid	A corrosive acid with vapors that are irritating to the respiratory system, eyes, and skin. Inhalation can cause tooth erosion. If ingested, causes severe internal irritation and damage that may cause death.	Potassium chlorate, potassium perchlorate, potassium permanganate.
Thionyl Chloride	Poison. May be fatal if inhaled. Vapor causes severe irritation to skin, eyes, and respiratory tract. May cause serious eye damage.	Reacts violently with water. Strong reducing agents, strong bases, and most common metals.
Toluene	Flammable liquid and vapor. May irritate skin, eyes, and respiratory tract. Aspiration hazard. Can cause central nervous system depression and nerve damage.	Halogens, combustible materials, acids, oxidizing materials, metal salts.

Chemical Name	Sources
2,5-Dimethoxybenzaldehyde	
Acetic Anhydride	http://www.state.nj.us/health/eoh/rtkweb/0005.pdf http://avogadro.chem.iastate.edu/MSDS/acetanhy htm
Acetone/ Ethyl Alcohol	http://avogadro.chem.iastate.edu/MSDS/acetone htm
Anhydrous Ammonia	http://www.ied.edu.hk/sci/safechem htm
Anthranilic Acid	http://www.basf.com/businesses/chemicals/intermediates/pdfs/anthran.pdf http://msds.pdc.cornell.edu/msds/msdsdod/a382/m190987 htm
Butylamine	http://www.state.nj.us/health/eoh/rtkweb/0280.pdf
Cyclohexanone	http://www.state.nj.us/health/eoh/rtkweb/0570.pdf
Ephedrine	http://physchem.ox.ac.uk/MSDS/EP/(-)-ephedrine_anhydrous html http://www.usg.edu/rtk/msds/MSDS0251.TXT
Ergometrine	http://www.medsafe.govt nz/Profs/Datasheet/e/Ergometrineinj.htm
Ethyl Acetate	http://www.state.nj.us/health/eoh/rtkweb/0841.pdf
Ethyl Ether	http://www.state.nj.us/health/eoh/rtkweb/0701.pdf http://www.matheson-trigas.com/msds/MAT08980.pdf
Ethylamine	http://www.state.nj.us/health/eoh/rtkweb/0847.pdf
Formamide	http://www.state.nj.us/health/eoh/rtkweb/0947.pdf
Formic Acid	http://www.state.nj.us/health/eoh/rtkweb/0948.pdf
Hydriodic Acid	http://www.matheson-trigas.com/msds/MAT11100.pdf
Hydrochloric Acid	http://www.mgindustries.com/msds/SubLookup.asp?SubName=11150 http://www.state.nj.us/health/eoh/rtkweb/1012.pdf
Iodine	http://www.ied.edu.hk/sci/safechem htm
Lithium Metal	http://www.rose-hulman.edu/che mistry/000000/000617.pdf
Methyl Ethyl Ketone	http://www.rose-hulman.edu/chemistry/000000/000816.pdf http://hillbrothers.com/msds/mek.htm
Methylamine	http://www.state.nj.us/health/eoh/rtkweb/1225.pdf
n-Acetylanthranilic Acid	http://physchem.ox.ac.uk/MSDS/AC/o-acetamidoanthranilic_acid.html
Nitroethane	http://www.rose-hulman.edu/chemistry/000000/000822.pdf
o-Toluidine	http://www.rose-hulman.edu/chemistry/000000/000848.pdf http://www.state.nj.us/health/eoh/rtkweb/1442.pdf
Phenethylamine	http://physchem.ox.ac.uk/MSDS/PH/phenethylamine http://hazard.com/msds/mf/baker/baker/files/p1872.htm
Phenyl-2-propanone (P2P)	http://www rose-hulman.edu/chemistry/000000/000809.pdf
Phenylacetic Acid	http://www.rose-hulman.edu/chemistry/000000/000087.pdf
Potassium Permanganate	http://www.rose-hulman.edu/chemistry/000000/000908.pdf
Pseudoephedrine	http://physchem.ox.ac.uk/MSDS/PS/(+)-pseudoephedrine html
Red Phosphorus	http://avogadro.chem.iastate.edu/MSDS/P-red htm
Safrole	http://www.state.nj.us/health/eoh/rtkweb/1642.pdf
Sodium Dichromate	http://physchem.ox.ac.uk/MSDS/SO/sodium_dichromate.html http://www.matheson-trigas.com/msds/MAT21190.pdf
Sodium Metal	http://www.matheson-trigas.com/msds/MAT20850.pdf
Thionyl Chloride	http://physchem.ox.ac.uk/MSDS/TH/thionyl_chloride.html http://www.udallas.edu/chemdept/hendrickson/MSDS/thionyl_chloride_ msds htm
Toluene	http://www.matheson-trigas.com/msds/MAT23590.pdf

This Page Intentionally Left Blank

Appendix K:
Methodology for Assessing Potential Consequences of Hazardous Waste Air Releases

The hazardous waste release scenarios for the DOJ COPS Office Methamphetamine Initiative, and the No Action Alternative were based on data collected during seizures of clandestine drug laboratories. The data collected included the types and quantities of chemicals found and the neighborhood categories and structure types encountered. The release scenario modeling approach and assumptions provides a screening type analysis of potential impacts from releases of selected chemicals to the indoor and outdoor air.

Selection of Chemicals for Analysis

According to the data, one of the most common substances recovered is ammonia gas. Ammonia gas is generally recovered in the form of compressed gas cylinders. Other common substances that are recovered at clandestine drug laboratories and that could cause fire and smoke are the flammable liquids acetone, toluene, and ethyl ether, which are recovered in containers of various sizes. Red phosphorus, which is incompatible with other chemicals commonly recovered at clandestine drug laboratories, including hydrochloric acid, is also one of the more common chemicals recovered. Red phosphorus may also decompose to the more highly reactive and spontaneously combustible yellow phosphorus form, or ignite if subjected to heat, friction, or static charge.[78] Potassium permanganate, a powerful oxidizer, may also be found at clandestine drug laboratories. Potassium permanganate is incompatible with all combustible organic chemicals (*e.g.,* acetone, toluene) and is also incompatible with hydrochloric and hydriodic acid[79]. Combination of these incompatible chemicals or decomposition of these chemicals could cause fire and smoke. Therefore, the quantitative analysis focuses on the effects of potential releases of toxic chemicals (*i.e.,* ammonia) to air.

Selection of Neighborhood Category/Structure Type

The neighborhood category/structure type scenarios discussed above were developed based on data collected for clandestine drug laboratory seizures, and were developed specifically to enable the assessment of a broad range of conditions related to potential hazardous waste releases in the Environmental Assessment. The scenarios selected for the hazardous waste release analyses are:

    a. Single Family House Scenario (indoor release)
    b. Single Family House Scenario (outdoor release)
    c. Multi-unit Residential Property Scenario
    d. Storage Unit Scenario (indoor storage unit)
    e. Storage Unit Scenario (outdoor release)

---

[78] Mallinckrodt, 1999. Material Safety Data Sheet, Phosphorus, Amorphous.
[79] J.T. Baker, 1999. Material Safety Data Sheet, Hydriodic Acid 40-60%.

f. Storage Unit Scenario (DEA Contractor)

Approach to Analyzing Air Releases

For air releases, the DOJ COPS Office conducted a quantitative analysis that includes modeling of the release and dispersion of the release. The DOJ COPS Office assumed that 100 kilograms of ammonia gas is involved in the release. In devising the release scenario, the DOJ COPS Office adopted the same definition used in Environmental Protection Agency's (EPA) Risk Management Program Rule, which states that a worst-case release is a release of the entire container of the substance over a ten-minute period.[80] For ammonia gas released indoors into a Single Family House, Multi-unit Residential Property *(e.g.,* apartment), storage unit or other structure, the DOJ COPS Office assumed that the gas initially becomes uniformly distributed within the structure. Therefore, the concentration of the ammonia within the structure is equal to the volume of the gas released divided by the volume of the structure. The DOJ COPS Office then determined the potential health effects of such concentrations based on established exposure limits such as the Emergency Response Planning Guide (ERPG) from the American Industrial Hygiene Association.[81] The ERPG-2 for ammonia is 150 parts per million (ppm). The ERPG-2 is the concentration below which nearly all people could be exposed to for a period of one hour without irreversible or other serious health effects or symptoms that would impair their ability to take protective action. ERPGs are oriented towards public exposure.

For an indoor release of ammonia gas, some portion of the ammonia would leave the building through windows, doors, and/or general ventilation systems. The DOJ COPS Office assumed that approximately 55 percent of the gas would leave the structure upon release. This factor was used in the EPA Offsite Consequence Analysis Guidance for gaseous releases inside a building.[82] The 55 percent factor was based on an analysis of *Risk Mitigation in Land Use Planning: Indoor Releases of Toxic Gases*[83]. For 100 kilograms of ammonia gas released into a building, approximately 55 kilograms would leave the building and disperse into the vicinity. The DOJ COPS Office examined the possibility of the ammonia released from the building entering a nearby house, apartment, or other building. The widely used ALOHA model (Area Locations of Hazardous Atmospheres) developed by the National Oceanic and Atmospheric Administration was used to assess the dispersion of ammonia and concentrations in nearby buildings.[84] **Caution must accompany the analysis results because dispersion predictions using any model are uncertain for the short distances to nearby structures.**

---

[80] Emergency Response Planning Guidelines (ERPG); developed by the American Industrial Hygiene Association, Fairfax, Virginia, 2002.

[81] Immediately Dangerous to Life or Health (IDLH); developed by the National Institute for Occupational Safety and Health (NIOSH) in *Occupational Health Guidelines for Chemical Hazards*, June 1994.

[82] EPA Offsite Consequence Analysis Guidance http://www.epa.gov/swercepp/ap-ocgu htm

[83] Porter, S.R. Risk Mitigation in Land Use Planning: Indoor Releases of Toxic Gases.

[84] Area Locations of Hazardous Atmospheres (ALOHA); developed by the National Oceanic and Atmospheric Administration and the Environmental Protection Agency. www.epa.gov/ceppo/cameo/aloha htm

For the releases of ammonia originating outside of a building, the DOJ COPS Office assumed that 100 percent of the release (100 kilograms) would be dispersed downwind from the point of the release. Likewise, for ammonia releases originating in an outdoor storage unit, the DOJ COPS Office assumed that 100 percent of the gas would escape through the ventilation system of the storage unit and would be dispersed downwind from the point of release.

Toxic Gas Release (Ammonia) Scenario Calculations and Results

Scenario a: Single Family House: Indoor Release

- Initial concentration inside the house is based on 100 kilograms of ammonia released into the house:

  Volume Ammonia = 100 kg * (m^3/0.713 kg) * (1ft^3/0.0283 m^3) = 4956 ft^3
  Ammonia Concentration = 4,956 ft^3/ 30,000 ft^3 * 1,000,000 = **160,000 ppm**

- Ammonia concentration at an adjoining house is based on 55% of the initial 100-kilogram release over a 10-minute period.

  ALOHA modeling results indicate that at a distance of 50 feet from the point of release, a human receptor (at an adjacent house) would be exposed to an ammonia concentration of 150 ppm, equivalent to the Emergency Response Planning Guidance (ERPG) level.

Scenario b: Single Family House: Outdoor Release

- Release concentration outdoors is based on 100 kilograms of ammonia released in the backyard of the house:

  ALOHA modeling results indicate that at a distance of 50 feet from the point of release, a human receptor (located at an adjacent house) would be exposed to an ammonia concentration greater than the Emergency Response Planning Guidance (ERPG) level. Human receptors located at houses 75 feet away from the point of release would be exposed to an ammonia concentration of 150 ppm, equivalent to the ERPG level.

Scenario c: Multi-unit Residential Property (e.g., Apartment Building) Scenario

- Initial concentration inside the apartment is based on 100 kilograms of ammonia released into the apartment:

  Volume Ammonia = 100 kg * (m^3/0.713 kg) * (1ft^3/0.0283 m^3) = 4956 ft^3
  Ammonia Concentration = 4,956 ft^3/ 15,000 ft^3 * 1,000,000 = **320,000 ppm**

- Ammonia concentration in adjoining apartment is based on 55% of the initial 100-kilogram release over a 10-minute period.

  ALOHA modeling results indicate that a human receptor in an adjacent apartment could be exposed to an ammonia concentration of approximately 6,400 ppm, a concentration far exceeding the 150 ppm Emergency Response Planning Guidance level.

Scenario d: Storage Unit Indoor Release

- Initial ammonia concentration inside the storage unit building is based on 100 kilograms of ammonia released into the storage unit and subsequently released into the building that the indoor storage unit is situated in:

  Volume Ammonia = 100 kg * (m^3/0.713 kg) * (1ft^3/0.0283 m^3) = 4956 ft^3
  Ammonia Concentration = 4,956 ft^3/ 60,000 ft^3 * 1,000,000 = **80,000 ppm**

  [Note: The DOJ COPS Office assumes that storage units may or may not be ventilated to outside of the building. The DOJ COPS Office also assumes that unventilated storage units are not designed to contain compressed gas releases. Therefore, it was assumed for this analysis that 100 percent of the 100-kilogram ammonia release escapes from an unventilated storage unit and into the building.]

- Ammonia concentration in adjoining residential area/commercial area based on 55% the initial 100-kilogram release over a 10-minute period.

  ALOHA modeling results indicate human receptors located in residential/commercial areas 50 feet from the point of release would be exposed to an ammonia concentration of 150 ppm, equivalent to the Emergency Response Planning Guidance level.

Scenario e: Storage Unit Outdoor Release

  ALOHA modeling results indicate that human receptors located in residential/commercial areas 50 feet from the point of release would be exposed to an ammonia concentration greater than the Emergency Response Planning Guidance (ERPG) level. Human receptors located 75 feet from the point of release would be exposed to an ammonia concentration of 150 ppm, equivalent to the Emergency Response Planning Guidance level.

Scenario f: DEA Contractor Transfer Station Indoor Release

- Initial ammonia concentration inside the transfer station is based on 100 kilograms of ammonia released into the transfer station

  Volume Ammonia = 100 kg * (m^3/0.713 kg) * (1ft^3/0.0283 m^3) = 4956 ft^3

Ammonia Concentration = 4,956 ft³/ 60,000 ft³ * 1,000,000 = **80,000 ppm**

- Ammonia concentration in adjacent house/commercial building is based on 55% of the initial 100-kilogram release over a 10-minute period.

ALOHA modeling results indicate that a human receptor located at a house/commercial building located 200 feet from the point of release would be exposed to an ammonia concentration lower than the 150 ppm Emergency Response Planning Guidance level.

Appendix L:
Water Quality Impact Analysis

The DOJ COPS Office assessed the potential impacts of releases of hazardous waste to surface water. A release could potentially result from a transportation or materials handling accident under the DOJ COPS Office Methamphetamine Initiative, or from a container breach or other inadvertent release from a container remaining in place under the No Action Alternative. The DOJ COPS Office assumed for the purposes of the water quality impact analysis that a maximum quantity of 100 kilograms of hazardous waste could be released to surface water as a result of such events.

The DOJ COPS Office based the analysis of potential impacts to water quality on the dispersion modeling methodology and river data presented in the USGS Paper *Prediction of Travel Time and Longitudinal Dispersion in Rivers and Stream* (USGS Report 96-4013).[85] The USGS report presents a model to predict the travel time and unit peak concentration of a contaminant released upstream of a water supply. The model can be used to estimate the rate of movement of a chemical release through a river reach, the rate of attenuation of the peak concentration over time, and the length of time for the contaminant plume to pass a particular point in the river. The USGS Report also presents tracer-response curve data obtained from soluble tracer (dye) injection studies conducted by USGS for 90 streams and rivers throughout the United States, for use in applying the model.

Data for the Apple River in northwestern Illinois and the Little Piney River in central Missouri are used in this Environmental Assessment for screening of water quality impacts of the Proposed Action. These rivers were selected for the screening analysis based upon their size (in terms of average volumetric flow rate), their location within grantee states, and the availability of a full data set in the USGS Report. Data for the tracer studies for these two rivers are shown in Table L.1. Larger rivers (e.g., the Mississippi River, the Missouri River) were not selected for screening analysis because any release into rivers of such large size would be diluted to levels below concern relatively quickly.

The tracer study data show the distance downstream of the dye injection point where the sampling was conducted and the volumetric flow rate of the river at the sampling point. The data also show the amount of time elapsed from the time of injection until the peak concentration was observed at the sampling point, and the amount of time elapsed until the concentration is reduced to ten percent of the observed peak concentration. The "unit peak concentration" in units of seconds^{-1} as calculated using the modeling methodology, is also reported. The unit peak concentration is the mass flux of solute (dye) at a given point in the river, in units of [milligrams per liter x liters per second, or milligrams per second] per unit of solute mass injected, in units of milligrams. This is calculated as

---

[85] Jobson, Harvey E., 1996. Prediction of Travel Time and Longitudinal Dispersion in Rivers and Streams, USGS Water Resources Investigations Report 96-4013, 1996.

$$C_{up} = C/M_r \times Q$$

Where C_{up} = unit peak concentration (seconds^{-1})
 C = observed concentration (milligrams per liter)
 M_r = mass of tracer recovered at a cross section (milligrams) and
 Q = river volumetric flow rate (liters per second)

Therefore the unit peak concentration may be used to estimate the peak concentration for a given flow rate and mass of solute (or contaminant) released.

Aquatic toxicity data for toluene were obtained from the USGS Report *Summary of Published Aquatic Toxicity Information and Water-Quality Criteria for Selected Volatile Organic Compounds* (USGS Report 97-563).[86] The USGS reported an EPA freshwater acute criteria/guideline for toluene of 17,500 micrograms per liter (ug/l.) Aquatic toxicity data for iodine were obtained from a Material Safety Data Sheets (MSDS) for iodine.[87] The MSDS reported a 24-hour LC_{50} for iodine of 440 ug/l. The LC_{50} represents the concentration at which 50 percent of an exposed aquatic species would experience mortality over the period of exposure. Iodine is not listed as a priority pollutant in the U.S. Clean Water Act. However, the Canadian Province of Ontario has developed an interim Provincial Water Quality Guideline (PWQG) of 100 ug/l for iodine.[88]

Iodine and toluene were selected for the screening water quality analysis based on the availability of aquatic toxicity data, the level of toxicity, and the quantities of these compounds recovered at clandestine drug laboratory sites. Toluene and iodine have been recovered from clandestine drug laboratories in quantities on the order of 100 kilograms for a single site. Toluene has higher aquatic toxicity than other organic compounds for which aquatic toxicity data are available (e.g., methyl ethyl ketone, acetone) and iodine has higher aquatic toxicity than other inorganic compounds for which aquatic toxicity data are available (e.g., potassium permanganate (manganese), phosphorus). Based on a density of 4.93 grams per milliliter, 100 kilograms of iodine is approximately equivalent to one five-gallon container, and 100 kilograms of toluene is approximately equivalent to one 30-gallon container, based on a density of 0.867 grams per milliliter.

As shown in Table L.1, in the event of a release of 100 kilograms of toluene to surface water, peak concentrations of toluene could exceed the freshwater acute criteria/guideline (FAC) for toluene under some circumstances. Using the USGS dispersion modeling approach, if a release occurred in the Apple River in the vicinity of the town of Apple River, Illinois at a high river flow rate (2.6 m^3/s) the peak concentration 1.9 kilometers from the point of release would be 69,300 ug/l, almost 400 percent of the FAC. The peak concentration would occur 1.3 hours after the time of release, and the concentration would

---

[86] USGS, 1997. Summary of Published Aquatic Toxicity Information and Water Quality Criteria for Selected Volatile Organic Compounds, USGS Open File Report 97-563, 1997.
[87] Safety Data Sheet – Iodine, 99.5%. CAS No. 7553-56-2, Personal Chemistry, Sweden, November 2000.
[88] Province of Ontario, 1994. Ontario Ministry of Environment and Energy, Policies, Guidelines, and Provincial Water Quality Objectives of the Ministry of Environment and Energy, July 1994 [reported in Review of Annex 1 of the Great Lakes Water Quality Agreement, Limno-Tech, Inc. March 14, 2001.]

be reduced to 10 percent of the peak concentration after 3.4 hours. If the release occurred at a low river flow rate (0.6 m^3/s) the peak concentration would be 27,700 ug/l, and would occur 3.7 hours after the time of release. The concentration would be reduced to 10 percent of the peak concentration after 7.8 hours.

In the event of a 100 kilogram release of iodine at high river flow rate, the peak iodine concentration would also be 69,300 ug/l at a distance of 1.9 kilometers from the point of release, as the modeling approach is independent of the characteristics of the substance released and only considers the quantity released and the characteristics of the river. However, this same concentration would be 15,700 percent of the reported LC$_{50}$ of 400 ug/l for iodine. The peak concentration would occur 1.3 hours after the time of release, and 3.4 hours after the time of release the concentration would be 10 percent of the peak concentration, but still 1,570 percent of the LC$_{50}$. Further downstream, at a point 35.6 kilometers from the point of release, the peak concentration would only be 2,313 ug/l, or 525 percent of the LC$_{50}$, and would occur 33 hours after the time of release. The concentration would fall to 10 percent of the peak concentration (231 ug/l, or 52.5 percent of the LC$_{50}$) 50 hours after the time of release. Therefore, an iodine concentration greater than 50 percent of the LC$_{50}$ would persist for approximately 18 hours at the 35.6 kilometer point.

Lower impacts are predicted for Little Piney Creek, for which tracer study data are only available for low flow (1.4 - 1.6 m^3/s) conditions. In the event of a 100-kilogram release of toluene, the peak concentration would be 19,850 ug/l (113 percent of the FAC for toluene) at a distance of 0.6 kilometers from the point of release, however the toluene concentration would be reduced to 1,985 ug/l (10 percent of the peak concentration) in less than 60 minutes. In the event of a 100-kilogram release of iodine, the peak concentration at the 0.6-kilometer point would be 4,500 percent of the LC$_{50}$, however, this concentration would persist for only a short time. At a point 5.2 kilometers from the point of release, the peak concentration would be approximately 2,410 ug/l (550 percent of the LC$_{50}$), however the concentration would be reduced to 240 ug/l (55 percent of the LC$_{50}$) within approximately 3 hours.

Note that the USGS modeling approach assumes that the release disperses immediately into the river (instantaneous slug release). A release of liquid toluene into a river would behave to some extent as an instantaneous source, however, iodine, being a crystalline solid that is only slightly soluble in water, may not immediately disperse into the river. This would somewhat reduce the magnitude of the peak concentrations from what are predicted in the model. Also, the USGS model does not consider chemical reactions that could take place between the contaminant released and water or other constituents. The contaminant released is assumed to disperse without reaction. Reactivity of iodine would also reduce the magnitude of the peak concentrations from the predicted concentrations.

Table L.1
Surface Water Release Screening Model

BASIC DATA

Inj No.		Little Piney Creek, Missouri				Apple River, Illinois					
		18	18	18	18	83	83	83	84	84	84
Km	Km	0.6	3.4	5.2	7.3	1.9	35.9	52	1.9	35.9	58.4
Q	m3/s	1.4	1.4	1.6	1.6	2.6	12.4	16.7	0.6	2.6	3.1
Tl	Hours	0.61	3.75	6.03	9.21	1	18.5	30.4	2.7	43.8	97.2
Tp	Hours	0.85	5.1	7.4	12	1.3	20.8	32.9	3.7	49.4	105.8
Tt	Hours	1.47	7.7	10.8	17.5	3.4	35.6	50.2	7.8	72.8	129.5
Qave	m3/s	4.4	4.4	4.4	4.4	0.7	3.8	5	0.7	3.8	5
Cup	s-1	873.2	138.1	106.1	75.1	485.2	87.9	60.5	193.8	36.5	29.7
Inj Mass	G	48	48	48	48	2400	2400	2400	450	450	450
R Ratio	Unitless	0.972	0.948	0.988	1	0.76	0.66	0.84	1.05	0.64	0.57

SCREENING MODEL CALCULATIONS

Release Mass	Mg	1.00E+08	1.00E+08	1.00E+08	1.00E+08	1.00E+08	1.00E+08	1.00E+08	1.00E+08	1.00E+08	1.00E+08
Qave	liter/s	4.40E+03	4.40E+03	4.40E+03	4.40E+03	7.00E+02	3.80E+03	5.00E+03	7.00E+02	3.80E+03	5.00E+03
Travel Time	s-1	873.2	138.1	106.1	75.1	485.2	87.9	60.5	193.8	36.5	29.7
Recovery Ratio	Unitless	1	1	1	1	1	1	1	1	1	1
C (peak) =	mg/l	19.85	3.14	2.41	1.71	69.31	2.31	1.21	27.69	0.96	0.59
C (peak) =	ug/l	19845	3139	2411	1707	69314	2313	1210	27686	961	594
C(peak)/FAC	Toluene	113.4%	17.9%	13.8%	9.8%	396.1%	13.2%	6.9%	158.2%	5.5%	3.4%
0.1 C(peak)/FAC	Toluene	11.3%	1.8%	1.4%	1.0%	39.6%	1.3%	0.7%	15.8%	0.5%	0.3%
C(peak)/LC50	Iodine	4510.3%	713.3%	548.0%	387.9%	15753.2%	525.7%	275.0%	6292.2%	218.3%	135.0%
0.1 C(peak)/LC50	Iodine	451.0%	71.3%	54.8%	38.8%	1575.3%	52.6%	27.5%	629.2%	21.8%	13.5%
Time to C (Peak)	Hours	0.85	5.10	7.40	12.00	1.30	20.80	32.90	3.70	49.40	105.80
Time to 10% C (Peak)	Hours	1.47	7.7	10.8	17.5	3.4	35.6	50.2	7.8	72.8	129.5
Distance to C (Peak)	Km	0.60	3.40	5.20	7.30	1.90	35.90	52.00	1.90	35.90	58.40

AQUATIC TOXICITY DATA

EPA Freshwater Acute Criteria (FAC)	Toluene	17,500ug/l
Aquatic Toxicity Criteria (LC50 24 hour)	Iodine	440ug/l

BASIC DATA KEY

Injection Number	Inj No.
Distance to Sampling Cross Section	Km
Flow Rate at Sampling Cross Section	Q
Time to Sampling Cross Section	Tl
Time to Peak Concentration	Tp
Time to 10% of Peak Concentration	Tt
Mean annual flow rate	Qave
Unit-peak Dye Concentration	Cup
Mass of Dye Injected	Inj Mass
Recovery Ratio	R Ratio

Sources:

USGS Water Resources Investigations Report 96-4013
Prediction of Travel time and Longitudinal Dispersion in Rivers and Streams
Harvey E. Johnson, USGS Water Resources Division, Reston Virginia http://water.usgs.gov/osw/pubs/disp/dispersion.html

Appendix M:
Methodology for Assessing Soil Quality Impacts

Potential impacts of the release of hazardous wastes to soil quality were assessed using generic soil screening levels (SSLs) developed by EPA for 110 chemicals. These include SSLs developed to assess potential ingestion of contaminated soils.[89] The generic SSLs, contained in Appendix A of the EPA Guidance Document, were derived by EPA using default values for the standardized equations in the Guidance Document, and are considered to be conservative and are likely to be protective for the majority of site conditions for contaminated soils. SSLs are used for evaluating soil contaminant levels at EPA hazardous waste remediation (Superfund National Priority List) sites and developing risk-based remediation strategies.

Of the hazardous wastes recovered from clandestine drug laboratory locations and listed in Table 6.3-1 of the Environmental Assessment, EPA has developed generic SSLs for soil ingestion for acetone, toluene, and chromium (a constituent of sodium dichromate.) The SSLs for acetone and toluene are higher than the generic SSLs for most of the other chemicals for which EPA developed generic SSLs. The DOJ COPS Office therefore believes that evaluation of soil concentrations against these SSLs would be representative of other hazardous wastes found at clandestine drug laboratories for which generic SSLs have not been developed.

For the purposes of assessing soil quality impacts, the DOJ COPS Office assumed that 100 kilograms of toluene or acetone and 2.5 kilograms of sodium dichromate (the maximum quantity discovered at a single clandestine drug laboratory location) could be released under the e removal action scenarios and transportation scenario under the Proposed Action, or from a container breach or other inadvertent release from a container remaining in place under the No Action Alternative. The calculated soil concentrations are the same for both Alternatives, because the DOJ COPS Office has assumed that the maximum amount of hazardous waste that could be released and the amount of soil area that such a release would cover are the same for each Alternative. The DOJ COPS Office assumed in calculating concentrations of hazardous waste in the soil that any release would cover an area of 10 square meters to a depth of one centimeter. The DOJ COPS Office calculated soil concentrations for each hazardous waste released to its soil ingestion SSL, as shown in Table M.1.

---

[89] EPA, 1996. U.S. EPA Soil Screening Guidance, EPA 540/R-96/018, July 1996, http://www.epa.gov/superfund/resources/soil

Table M.1
Soil Hazardous Waste Screening Release Calculations

Release Parameters	Toluene		Acetone		Sodium Dichromate	
Spill Amount	100	kilograms	100	kilograms	2.5	kilograms
Spill Amount	1.00E+08	milligrams	1.00E+08	milligrams	2.50E+06	milligrams
Spill Area	10	m^2	10	m^2	10	m^2
Spill Depth	1	cm	1	cm	1	cm
Spill Depth	0.1	m	0.1	m	0.1	m
Soil Density	1.5	kilograms/liter	1.5	kilograms/liter	1.5	kilograms/liter
Soil Density	1500	kilograms/ m^3	1500	kilograms/ m^3	1500	kilograms/ m^3
Soil Mass Amount	1500	kilograms	1500	kilograms	1500	kilograms
Soil Concentration	66,667	mg/kg	66,667	mg/kg	331	mg Cr/kg*
Generic Ingestion SSLs	16,000	mg/kg	7,800	mg/kg	390	mg/kg
Soil Concentration / SSL	416%		854%		84%	

Notes:
The molecular weights of $Na_2Cr_2O_7$ (261.97) and Cr (51.996) were used for the above calculations.
SSL = Soil Screening Level
* $Na_2Cr_2O_7$ concentration in soil is 1667mg/kg of which 19.85% (or 331 mg/kg) is due to Cr
Source: EPA, 1996. U.S. EPA Soil Screening Guidance, EPA 540/R-96/018, July 1996,
http://www.epa.gov/superfund/resources/soil

www.ingramcontent.com/pod-product-compliance
Lightning Source LLC
Chambersburg PA
CBHW081456170526
45166CB00008B/2448